ULTIMATE

QUESTIONS
&ANSWERS

SCIENCE

AUTUMN
PUBLISHING

CONTENTS:

WHAT IS MATTER?

All substance in the Universe, from the tiniest speck of dust to the largest star, is matter. All matter is made up of tiny pieces called atoms. Scientists once thought that atoms were the smallest things in the Universe—that they were like tiny balls that could never be split or destroyed. In fact, they are more like clouds of energy made up of mostly empty space containing simpler elements called particles. Particles smaller than an atom are subatomic particles.

Stars, dust, gases—everything in the Universe is matter.

WHO FIRST SPLIT AN ATOM?

In 1919 the physicist Ernest Rutherford proved that the atom was not one solid ball, but made up of different parts. He broke down nitrogen atoms into oxygen and hydrogen, later redefining the hydrogen molecule as a proton.

Ernest Rutherford

Big? WHAT ARE PARTICLES MADE UP OF?

Scientists believe that there are two basic kinds of particles: quarks and leptons. Electrons, the negatively charged particles that buzz around inside an atom, are leptons. Positively charged protons, and neutrons that have no charge, are found clustered in the center of an atom, in the nucleus. These protons and neutrons are made from different "flavors" of quark. There are actually six different kinds of quark but only two—"up" quarks and "down" quarks—are long-lived, and these are what protons are made of.

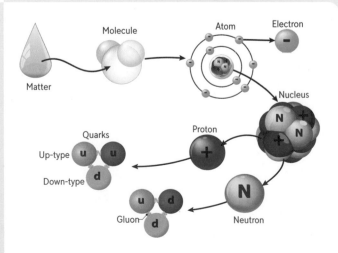

Matter—from molecule to quark

Matter · Molecule · Atom · Electron · Nucleus · Proton · Neutron

Quarks
Up-type u u
Down-type d
Gluon u d d

WHAT IS A NUCLEUS?

Most of an atom is empty space, but at its center is a tiny area called the nucleus. This contains two kinds of nuclear particles—neutrons with no electrical charge and protons with a positive electrical charge.

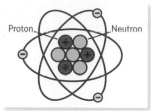

The nucleus of an atom

DO ATOMS EXIST ALONE?

Atoms rarely exist alone. They usually join together in small groups called molecules. Hydrogen atoms, for instance, exist in pairs or joined to other atoms. A molecule of hydrogen gas H_2 is made up of a pair of hydrogen atoms. A water molecule H_2O is a pair of hydrogen atoms joined together with an oxygen atom.

A molecule of water (H_2O)

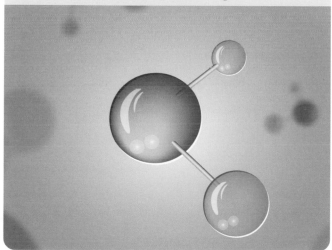

Rapid-FIRE?

WHAT ARE PROTONS MADE OF?

A proton is a cluster of three quarks, held together by gluons.

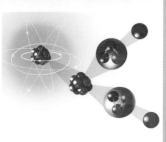

Proton

WHAT ARE THE PARTICLES IN A HELIUM ATOM?

Helium has two electrons, protons, and neutrons, with one proton and neutron pair for each electron.

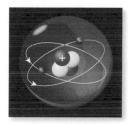

Helium atom

WHICH IS THE SMALLEST ATOM?

The hydrogen atom.

Hydrogen atom

HOW MANY SUBATOMIC PARTICLES ARE THERE?

Currently, scientists know of more than 200 kinds of subatomic particles.

HOW IS AN ATOM HELD TOGETHER?

The first of the three forces that hold an atom together is the electrical attraction between negative electrons and positive protons. Then there are the strong and weak nuclear forces that hold particles of the nucleus together. These two, and gravity, are the basic forces that hold the atom together.

An atom

WHAT IS FORCE?

Force is simply what is applied to push or pull something. An object has a natural tendency not to move unless it is forced to; force is what opposes the non-movement. Force is also what helps to stop things from moving. A moving car can be stopped only with force.

Applying force to lift weights in a gym

Big? IS THERE SOMETHING LIKE A UNIVERSAL FORCE?

Earth's gravitational force

Earth revolves around the Sun; it also rotates on its axis. Yet, we can stand and be still on Earth. When a coin or a ball is tossed up, it falls back to the ground. This is because of gravity—the force of attraction that holds the Universe together. Every bit of matter in the Universe has its own gravitational pull and attracts every other bit of matter. The strength of the pull depends on how massive things are and the distance between them.

WHAT IS A CHAIN REACTION?

When two objects collide, their combined momentum remains the same if nothing else interferes. But, if one object loses momentum (motion and energy), this momentum must be passed on to the other object, making it move. This is a chain reaction.

Chain reaction

WHAT IS A TURNING FORCE?

When something is fixed in one place, called a fulcrum, and is pushed or pulled elsewhere, it moves around the fulcrum. When you push a door shut, that push is the turning force, and the hinge is the fulcrum.

Pushing open a door

WHAT DID ISAAC NEWTON DISCOVER?

He discovered the force of gravity. He also explained the link between force and motion with his three laws of motion. These three laws explain a lot about movement—be it the flowering of a bud or a moving truck. Newton lived in the 17th century.

Isaac Newton

Satellite

Orbit

Gravity

Orbit

WHY DO THINGS GO AROUND?

An object will keep on moving in a straight line if only one force is involved. When another force comes into play to pull it in toward a fixed center point, it causes the object to change its path and go around in a circle.

Earth's gravitational force keeps the satellite moving around it.

Rapid-FIRE ?

DOES FORCE DEPEND ON THE MASS OF AN OBJECT?

It depends on both the mass and acceleration.

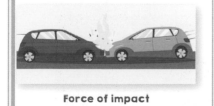

Force of impact

HOW MANY DIFFERENT KINDS OF FORCES CAN ACT UPON AN OBJECT?

There are six different forces: normal, applied, friction, tension, spring, and resistance.

Friction

Normal

Applied

Resistance

Spring

Tension

Types of force

IS MAGNETISM A FORCE?

Yes. It pushes or pulls.

Magnetic force field

WHAT WAS NEWTON'S BREAKTHROUGH?

In 1687 the English scientist Sir Isaac Newton realized something quite amazing—that all movement in the Universe is governed by three simple rules. These three rules, which are now called Newton's laws of motion, were tested over and over again by many scientists, until it was finally agreed that they are true.

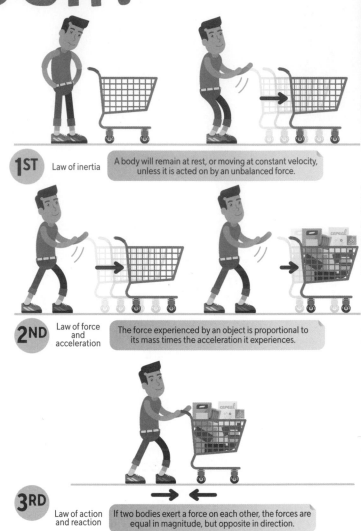

1ST Law of inertia — A body will remain at rest, or moving at constant velocity, unless it is acted on by an unbalanced force.

2ND Law of force and acceleration — The force experienced by an object is proportional to its mass times the acceleration it experiences.

3RD Law of action and reaction — If two bodies exert a force on each other, the forces are equal in magnitude, but opposite in direction.

Newton's laws of motion

Rapid-FIRE ?

WHAT IS THE MOVEMENT OF A PENDULUM CALLED?

Oscillation.

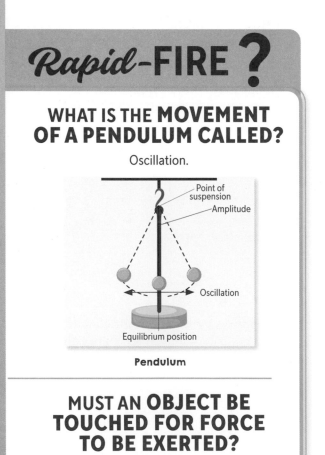

Point of suspension
Amplitude
Oscillation
Equilibrium position

Pendulum

MUST AN OBJECT BE TOUCHED FOR FORCE TO BE EXERTED?

No. Forces such as gravity or magnetism don't require any kind of contact to be made.

WHAT IS DISPLACEMENT?

It is the distance moved by an object in a particular direction.

WHAT IS THE THEORY OF RELATIVITY?

This theory explains how space and time can be measured only in comparison to something else. This means that the measurements will change depending on how fast you are moving!

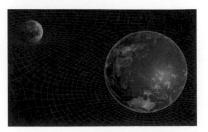

Measuring space and time

CAN YOU MOVE AN OBJECT WITHOUT IT RESISTING?

No, because of inertia, which is the resistance an object offers to a force trying to move it or change its velocity. How much resistance an object offers depends on its mass. Even a moving object can have inertia until any force stops or changes its velocity.

Pull

Push

Overcoming inertia

Feeling the push back

DOES EVERY ACTION HAVE A REACTION?

Yes, this is Newton's third law, which states that for every action there is an equal and opposite reaction. What this means is that whenever something moves, a force also pushes back in the opposite direction. For instance, when you push your legs forward in water, the water pushes back with equal force.

Big?
WHAT ARE THE FIRST TWO LAWS OF MOTION?

Newton's first law states that an unmoving object will remain unmoving, and a moving object will keep moving until an external force acts upon them. This means that in a space where there is no gravity, an object will stay where it is placed, and if it is thrown it will keep on moving forever. Newton's second law states that an object will move faster if more force is applied to it, and that more force is needed to move an object that has greater mass. For example, if a large boulder and a small boulder were placed at the top of a slope, while the smaller boulder would gain speed while rolling down, more force would be needed to start the bigger boulder rolling.

A falling apple is believed to have led Newton to connect gravity and motion.

WHAT IS THE DIFFERENCE BETWEEN MASS AND WEIGHT?

Mass is the amount of matter in an object. It is the same wherever you measure it, even on the Moon. Weight is a measure of the force of gravity on an object. It varies according to where you measure it.

Newton's theory of gravity

WHAT IS TERMINAL VELOCITY?

When a stone falls, the speed (velocity) at which it drops increases at a rate of 32 ft per second. But, as its speed increases, resistance from the air it pushes against also increases until a balance is reached. Once that happens, the speed at which the stone continues to fall steadies. This is called terminal velocity. This is why a parachute floats gently down to the ground.

Balancing weight and air resistance

Big? HOW DOES GRAVITY PULL US DOWN?

Earth's gravity pulls everything down.

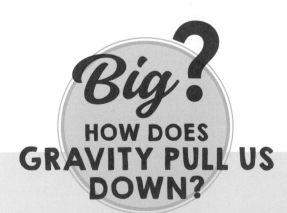

Gravity is an invisible force of attraction that exists between every bit of matter in the Universe, even between Earth and the Sun. The strength of the pull of gravity depends on the mass of the objects involved and the distance between them. For example, if you jump off a wall, the Earth pulls you toward the ground. At the same time, you pull the Earth toward you but, because you are tiny in relation to the Earth, you move a lot while the Earth barely moves at all.

WHAT HAPPENS TO ASTRONAUTS WHEN THEY COME BACK TO EARTH?

There is no gravity in space. So astronauts' bodies don't have to work as hard as on Earth. Because of this the muscles shrink slightly and lose some strength. The heart also doesn't have to pump as hard in space. When back on Earth, astronauts' bodies need to readjust to functioning with gravity and this can take some days.

Checking physical performance after spaceflight

WHY CAN WE JUMP HIGHER ON THE MOON?

The Moon is much smaller than the Earth, so the pull of its gravity is much weaker. Astronauts weigh six times less on the Moon than they do on Earth, and can jump much higher!

WHY ARE SATELLITES NOT PULLED DOWN TO EARTH?

As objects zip through space, Earth's gravity tries to pull them down to its surface. At the same time, the speed at which they are traveling exerts its own force, pulling them away. So satellites end up zooming around Earth at the exact distance where the two forces are equal. This is their path of orbit.

Satellite in space

Rapid-FIRE ?

WILL A BALL WEIGHING 5 IBS FALL FASTER THAN ONE WEIGHING 2 lbs?

Both will hit the ground at the same time because gravity accelerates every object at the same rate.

Gravity pulls both objects equally.

HOW MUCH WOULD YOU WEIGH ON JUPITER?

Almost two and half times what you weigh on Earth.

Jupiter

IS GRAVITATIONAL FORCE VERY STRONG?

Though it holds the Universe together, gravity is still the weakest known force!

WHAT IS MECHANICAL ADVANTAGE?

There are always two forces involved in a load-moving machine: a "load," which is the force the machine is designed to overcome; and the "effort," which is the force needed to move the load. A machine reduces the amount of effort needed to move a load, and that reduced effort is known as "mechanical advantage."

Effort

Using a simple lever to move a load

The gearbox of a car

Big? HOW DOES A GEAR WORK?

Gears reduce effort by spreading it out over a greater distance using special wheels called cogs that have teeth around the edge. Pairs of wheels of different sizes turn each other, with the teeth meshing for a stronger, nonslip grip. The number of times the driving wheel turns the driven wheel is called the gear ratio. In a ratio of 5:1, the driving wheel turns five times for each time the driven wheel turns. With a big gear ratio, the driven wheel turns more slowly relative to the driving wheel, but it turns with more force. With a small gear ratio, the driven wheel turns with less force, but turns faster.

DOES APPLYING FORCE ALWAYS MAKE THINGS MOVE?

Even an immovable object has various forces acting on it. The study of things that do not move is called statics. The study of the way objects move when force is applied is called dynamics.

A moving car and a static mountain

WHAT DOES A LEVER DO?

A lever is a simple mechanical device that makes it easier to move a load. A rod fixed at one point, yet free to swivel, is a lever. The fixed point is the fulcrum. If you push on one end of the rod, your effort can be used to move a load on the part of the rod that is on the other side of the fulcrum. The farther away from the fulcrum you apply your effort, and the closer the load is to the fulcrum on the other side, the more your effort will be multiplied.

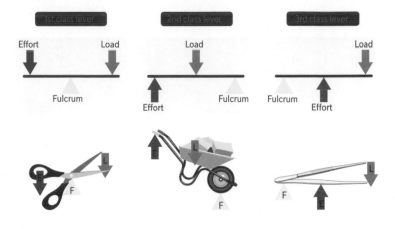

Different types of levers

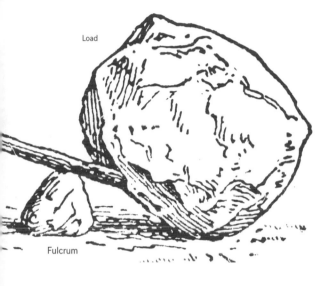

HOW IS "WORK" DEFINED?

The total amount of effort put into moving something is called "work." This means that work is the force used multiplied by the distance the load moves. Work is measured in joules. So if one newton (measurement of force) was used to move the load around one yard then one joule of work is done.

Moving a load

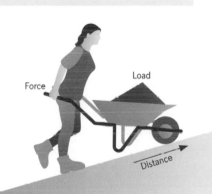

Rapid-FIRE ?

Crowbar as a lever

HOW DOES A CROWBAR WORK?

Through the fulcrum located between the load and the effort.

WHAT DOES CHANGING GEARS MEAN?

Selecting the gears for the best combination of force and speed.

Gearshift in a car

Bicycle chain and gears

WHAT IS THE ROLE OF A CHAIN IN A BICYCLE?

The chain connects the pedal wheel and cogs of the gears.

HOW DO ENGINES WORK?

Most engines work by burning fuel to make gases that expand rapidly when they are heated. In cars and trains, the hot gases expand inside what is called a combustion chamber, and push against a piston or a turbine (a kind of fan). In rockets, the burning gases swell and push against the whole engine as they shoot out of the back.

A car engine

WHAT IS **HORSEPOWER?**

It indicates how powerful an engine is by comparing it to the number of horses it would take to do the same amount of work in a minute: an eight horsepower engine can generate power equal to the strength of eight horses.

A horse-powered car in Manchester, New Hampshire, USA, in 1877

Big **?**
WHAT IS A FOUR-STROKE ENGINE?

Four-stroke, internal combustion engine

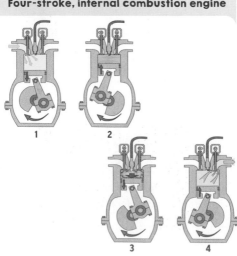

1   2

3   4

Most car engines are four-stroke. That means each piston goes up and down four times for each power stroke. The power stroke generates force to move the car. First, a valve opens to allow fuel to be drawn in by the piston as it descends. Second, the valve closes and the piston rises, squeezing the fuel. Third, a spark lights the fuel, which expands and thrusts the piston down a tube called a cylinder. Here, it turns a rod called a crank, which turns the wheels. Fourth, the piston rises again to push the burned gases out of the exhaust.

HOW DO JET ENGINES WORK?

Jet engines suck in air through the front. This burns with aviation fuel, expands very rapidly, and shoots out from the back of the engine. In accordance with Newton's third law of motion, this creates a major thrust that pushes the plane forward.

Jet engine

WHAT IS ACCELERATION?

Acceleration is how fast something gains speed. The greater the force and the lighter the object, the greater the acceleration will be. That is why sports cars go so fast—the engine is very powerful while the car is relatively small. A decrease in speed is called deceleration.

F1 race car

WHAT IS HYDRAULIC POWER?

Fluids such as water cannot be squashed or compressed. When we squeeze fluid through a pipe it pushes out forcefully through the other end. Hydraulic power uses fluid-filled pipes to drive things smoothly. Though hydraulic means "to be operated by water," most hydraulic systems use oil to prevent rusting.

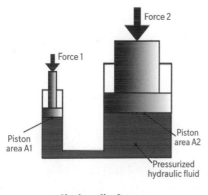

Force 2
Force 1
Piston area A1
Piston area A2
Pressurized hydraulic fluid

Hydraulic force

Rapid-FIRE ?

WHAT ARE THE MAIN LIQUID FUELS ARE USED IN CARS?

Gasoline, diesel, liquid petroleum gas (LPG), and compressed natural gas (CNG).

Fuel pump

Battle tank

HOW POWERFUL ARE BATTLE TANK ENGINES?

They generate between 1,000 and 1,500 horsepower.

WHO INVENTED JET ENGINES?

Frank Whittle and Pabst von Ohain.

Frank Whittle

Pabst von Ohain

WHAT GAS COMBINES WITH LIQUID FUEL AS IT BURNS IN A CAR ENGINE?

Oxygen.

WHAT IS MAGNETISM?

Magnetism is an invisible natural force generated by some metals, called magnets. The force affects a certain area around each magnet, which is called its magnetic field. Every magnet has two poles: a north pole and a south pole. If the same poles of two magnets meet, they push away from each other; if opposite poles meet, they pull together.

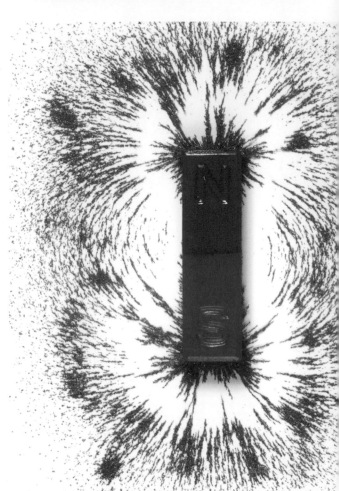

Magnet and its magnetic field

Big? IS EARTH A MAGNET?

Earth is a giant magnet, and it behaves almost as if there were a giant magnet running through its middle, from pole to pole. Earth's magnetic force is generated right at its core, which is composed of iron and nickel. Since the outer core is liquid and the inner core solid, they rotate at different speeds. The currents produced by these rotations turn the core into a giant electromagnet. Earth's magnetism not only affects magnets on its surface, but it also affects electrically charged particles out in space. The region of space it influences is called the magnetosphere.

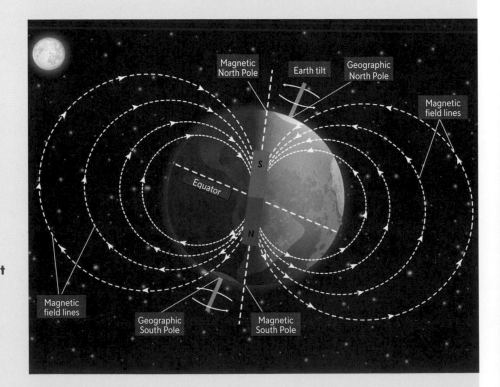

Earth as a magnet

Magnetic North Pole

Earth tilt

Geographic North Pole

Magnetic field lines

S

Equator

Magnetic field lines

N

Geographic South Pole

Magnetic South Pole

WHAT IS A **MAGNETIC POLE?**

The powerful pull that magnets exert is especially strong at each end of the magnet. These two powerful extremities are called poles. Opposite poles of magnets attract each other and like poles repel—two north or two south poles will push each other away but a north and south pole will stick together.

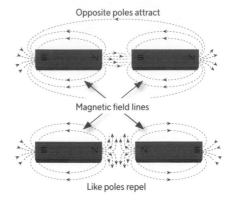
Opposite poles attract

Magnetic field lines

How magnets behave

Like poles repel

WHAT IS A **MAGNETIC DOMAIN?**

No matter how many times you cut a magnet in half, you will get two little magnets, each with a north and south pole. This is because magnetic materials are made of tiny groups of atoms called domains, which are like mini magnets in themselves.

CAN **IRON LOSE ITS MAGNETIC PROPERTY?**

Yes, at above 1,400 °F, which is known as the Curie temperature. Above this, heat disrupts the spontaneous arrangement of atomic magnets in iron and it loses its magnetic property.

WHY DO THE **AURORAS OCCUR?**

Right over the poles is a gaping hole in Earth's magnetic field where the lines of magnetic force funnel inward. Every now and then, charged particles from the Sun stream in through the hole and crash violently into air molecules, making them dance and glow brightly as a phenomenon called an aurora.

Aurora in the night sky

Rapid-FIRE?

WHY IS THE **MAGNETOSPHERE IMPORTANT?**

Without its protection, Earth would be exposed to the solar wind, a lethal stream of charged particles speeding out from the Sun.

Solar wind deflected by Earth's magnetosphere

WHAT IS THE **MAGNETIC DIP?**

Magnets not only swivel to point north but also point downward. This is called magnetic dip.

Compass

WHO MADE THE **FIRST MAGNETIC COMPASS?**

The ancient Chinese were probably the first.

WHAT IS ENERGY?

Energy takes many forms: energy from heat boils water, keeps us warm, and drives engines; chemical energy fuels cars; electrical energy keeps lights glowing—and light is also a form of energy. Almost every form of energy can be converted into another, but whatever form it is in, energy is essentially the capacity to make something happen.

Putting energy to work

WHAT ARE ALTERNATIVE SOURCES OF ENERGY?

Clean, renewable sources of energy that provide an alternative to fossil fuels are solar, hydro, wind, biomass, and geothermal. Magnets are also being used to increase efficiency and generate power.

Harnessing energy from the wind and Sun

Big? IS THE SUN A STRONG SOURCE OF ENERGY?

Sun and Earth

As much as 53 percent of the Sun's energy is reflected or absorbed by Earth's atmosphere before it can reach the ground. However, just one hour of the remaining 47 percent of the Sun's energy is enough to generate enough power for the entire world to use for a whole year! Some solar panels generate heat as water that is sandwiched between sheets of glass heated by the Sun. Solar cells are light-sensitive chemicals that generate an electric current when hit by sunlight.

IS **NUCLEAR ENERGY RENEWABLE?**

No. Nuclear energy is nonrenewable, because uranium and plutonium, the elements used to generate the heat to move the turbines, are limited resources. But the process of nuclear fission uses uranium and plutonium so slowly that it will be a long time before they run out.

Nuclear power station

CAN **FOSSIL FUELS MEET THE WORLD'S ENERGY NEEDS?**

Almost 90 percent of the energy used today comes from fossil fuels. About 40 percent is from oil, 27 percent from coal and 21 percent from natural gas. Because these energy sources were created over millions of years, however, they are nonrenewable and will eventually be used up. In addition, they pollute the air, contributing to climate change.

Offshore oil platform

WHAT IS **HYDROELECTRIC POWER?**

Hydroelectric power is an alternative source of energy generated by moving water. Most hydroelectric power stations are built inside big dams, which build up water pressure to turn the turbines that generate electricity.

Hydroelectric dam

WHAT IS **GEOTHERMAL ENERGY?**

Energy generated from hot water and steam that finds its way up from deep inside the earth.

Geothermal power plant, Iceland

HOW FAST DOES **ELECTRICITY TRAVEL?**

Around 18,000 miles per second, which is almost as fast as the speed of light.

City lights

WHICH COUNTRIES ARE THE **LARGEST PRODUCERS OF HYDROPOWER?**

The United States, Russia, Canada, Brazil, and China are the top five producers.

WHAT IS HEAT?

Heat is a form of energy generated by the movement of molecules that are present inside matter. The faster the molecules move, the more heat is generated and the hotter the object becomes. When we feel the heat of a fire, we are actually feeling millions of fast-moving molecules of air that are being heated up by millions of even faster-moving molecules in the fire.

Burning wood to generate heat to boil water

Vostok research station, Antarctica

WHAT IS THE LOWEST TEMPERATURE EVER RECORDED?

In natural weather conditions, it was a chilling -128.7 °F, at the Russian scientific station at Vostok, Antarctica. But the lowest artificially made temperatures ever achieved have been in laboratories—just a few thousandths of a degree above absolute zero, which is more than 10,000 times colder than deep space.

Rapid-FIRE?

Ice cubes in water

AT WHAT TEMPERATURES DOES WATER FREEZE AND BOIL?

Water freezes at 32 °F and boils at 212 °F.

Pyrometer

WHICH INSTRUMENT IS USED TO MEASURE VERY HIGH TEMPERATURES?

A pyrometer.

WHICH IS THE FASTEST WAY HEAT IS TRANSFERRED?

Radiation.

WHAT HELPS HEAT MOVE EASILY?

A heat conductor.

WHAT DOES NOT ALLOW HEAT TO MOVE EASILY?

An insulator.

WHAT ARE CONDUCTION, CONVECTION, AND RADIATION?

There are three ways in which heat spreads. Conduction is through direct contact between substances—a little like a relay race when moving hot particles knock into colder ones and transfer heat. Convection is when warm particles rise through cool air like a hot-air balloon. Radiation happens when heat spreads through a space without any visible direct contact between particles.

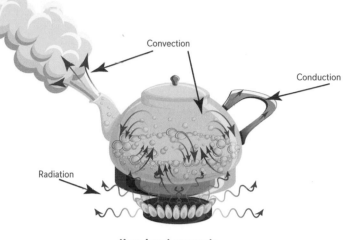

How heat spreads

WHAT IS **ABSOLUTE ZERO?**

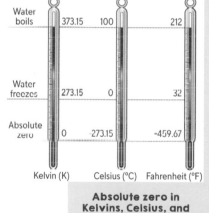

Absolute zero in Kelvins, Celsius, and Fahrenheit

Absolute zero is the coldest possible temperature—a temperature at which all molecules stop moving and no heat is being generated at all. This happens at -459.67 °F. It is also measured as zero on the Kelvin scale.

Mercury thermometer

WHAT IS THE **HIGHEST TEMPERATURE EVER RECORDED?**

Furnace Creek, California

The official highest, natural surface air temperature ever recorded in the world is 134 °F, in Furnace Creek, California, USA. A sizzling five trillion kelvins—the temperature of the Universe just after the Big Bang—was generated by the Large Hadron Collider machine in Geneva, Switzerland.

Big? WHAT IS TEMPERATURE AND HOW IS IT MEASURED?

Temperature indicates how hot something is—how fast its molecules are moving. A thermometer is used to measure temperature. Most thermometers contain a tube of liquid, such as mercury. The liquid expands with heat and its level in the tube rises, indicating the temperature. Everyday temperatures are measured in degrees—Celsius or Fahrenheit.

WHAT IS ELECTRICITY?

Electricity is a form of energy that is linked with magnetism. Electricity starts with atoms and tiny parts of each atom called electrons. Electrons have a negative charge, while protons (found in the nucleus) are positive. It is the combined attraction of billions of tiny electrons to billions of tiny protons that creates electricity.

Lighting up the modern city

Big? HOW DO ELECTRICITY AND MAGNETS AFFECT EACH OTHER?

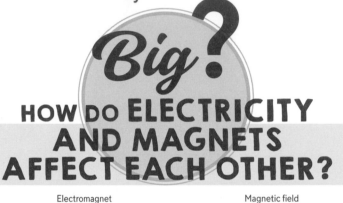

Electromagnet

Battery

Magnetic field

Current out

N

Coil carrying electric current

Current in

S

Making an electromagnet

When a coil of electrical wire is moved near a magnet—or a magnet is moved near an electrical wire—the magnetic force draws electrons through the wire, creating an electrical current. Just as moving magnets creates electricity, an electrical current can make a magnet move. When a current is passed through a wire coiled around an iron bar, it turns the bar into a very powerful magnet, called an electromagnet, or solenoid. This whole exchange of energy between electrical charge and magnetic force is called electromagnetism.

WHAT IS STATIC CHARGE?

A buildup of electrons where there is no possibility of movement or a current creates static electricity. This collection of electrons looks for something with a lower charge to jump onto, which is why you sometimes get a shock when you touch a doorknob.

Static electricity can make your hair stand up.

WHY DOES LIGHTNING FLASH?

As raindrops and ice crystals inside a thundercloud are flung around, they lose or gain electrons to become electrically charged. Lighter, positively charged particles gather high up, while heavy, negatively charged particles build up at the base of the cloud. The negatively charged particles are discharged as lightning.

A flash of lightning

WHAT IS POTENTIAL DIFFERENCE?

For an electrical current to flow, there has to be a difference in charge between two points in the circuit. This is "potential difference," and it is measured in volts. A current flows from higher to lower voltage.

Rapid-FIRE ?

WHAT DID BENJAMIN FRANKLIN PROVE?

That lightning is a form of electricity.

Benjamin Franklin

DOES ALL CURRENT FLOW IN THE SAME WAY?

Direct current (DC) electrons flow steadily in one direction; alternating current (AC) electrons vibrate back and forth from positive to negative.

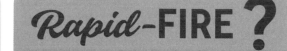

Direct current   **Alternating current**

DOES ELECTRICAL CURRENT FLOW?

Yes, when an electrical charge flows through a wire in a continuous stream, it forms a current. For a current to flow, it needs an unbroken circular path, or circuit. Electrons that have broken free from their atoms pass the current on as they hit against each other like a row of marbles.

HOW DO ELECTRIC MOTORS WORK?

They work by sending an electric current through a wire coiled around a magnet. The surge of electricity through the coil makes the magnet turn.

Electric motor

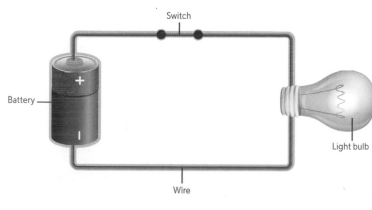

Switch

Battery

Light bulb

Wire

An electric circuit

WHAT ARE ELECTRONICS?

Electronics are systems with tiny circuits that use electricity to send signals and process information. Modern technologies use electronics to control everything from microwave ovens to televisions. Inside every device are lots of circuits that continually switch on and off, telling the device what to do. These switches can be programmed to work automatically.

Electronic circuit board

HOW DO COMPUTERS REMEMBER?

Computers work electronically. Some of the computer's memory, called the ROM (read-only memory) is built into microchips that contain a million or more transistors—the brain of the computer. Random-access memory (or RAM) circuits take in new data and instructions. Data can also be stored as magnetic patterns on removable disks such as DVDs or USB drives.

Microchips in a computer's motherboard

Big? WHAT IS VIRTUAL REALITY?

Experiencing virtual reality

It is electronically possible to build images so perfect that they create an illusion of reality; this is known as virtual reality (VR). Customized headset lenses present a slightly different view from each eye even makes it possible to experience virtual reality in 3D, with changing views that project the impression of moving through real space. Special gloves and other devices help in controlling movement to enhance the illusion. Besides boosting the experience of video games, VR devices now enable us to experience various tasks that are otherwise too difficult or dangerous, such as exploring inside a human body or a shipwreck in the ocean.

WHAT IS A FRACTAL?

Never-ending patterns generated by computers from simple mathematical calculations that are repeated over and over are called fractals. Fractal patterns are extremely familiar since they are found all over nature—the branches of a tree divide out into more branches, which divide into more and so on.

Fractals in nature

WHAT IS A SEMICONDUCTOR?

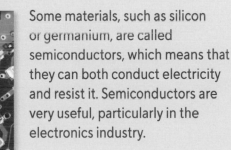

Some materials, such as silicon or germanium, are called semiconductors, which means that they can both conduct electricity and resist it. Semiconductors are very useful, particularly in the electronics industry.

A semiconductor

WHAT IS A SILICON CHIP?

An electronic circuit implanted in a small crystal of semiconducting silicon. Dozens, even thousands of tiny transistors can be joined together in a single integrated circuit packed inside a single tiny slice of silicon. Because they can be designed for various specialized processes, today, these chips power all kinds of devices, from microwave ovens to supercomputers.

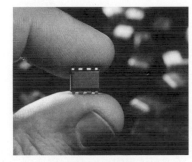

A silicon chip

Rapid-FIRE ?

WHO BUILT THE FIRST COMPUTER?

Charles Babbage, in the 1830s.

Charles Babbage

WHAT IS CYBERSPACE?

An artificial environment created by computers.

Cyberspace is accessed through a computer.

WHO FIRST DEVELOPED THE INTERNET?

The American military.

WHAT ARE THE USES OF ELECTRICITY?

In the late 19th century, scientists discovered how to harness electricity and use it as a source of energy. Since then, the world has come to rely on electricity more and more. Today, electricity is used to power lighting, heating, industry, transportation, communications, computers, and much more.

Charging an electric car

Electricity pylons

Big? HOW IS ELECTRICITY TRANSMITTED?

Electricity can be generated in power stations and then sent to where it is needed through big cables buried underground or strung on high towers called pylons. Electricity is transmitted through these cables at a very high voltage (high pressure) to make sure it reaches its destination or distribution centers. The current, however, is very low. When it reaches the distribution centers a balancing is carried out—the voltage is reduced and the current increased by transformers. Local cables then distribute the electricity to the final destination.

HOW DOES A LIGHT BULB WORK?

A light bulb has a very thin filament of tungsten wire inside a closed glass bulb filled with argon or nitrogen gas. When a current is passed through the thin wire, resistance causes the wire to heat up and glow, producing light.

Glowing filament in a light bulb

Portable generator

HOW DOES A GENERATOR WORK?

An electricity generator uses mechanical energy to create electrical energy. Many generators use electromagnetic induction in which a conducting wire, such as copper wire, is coiled around inside a magnet. This causes electrons in the wire to move and generate electricity.

WHAT IS LCD?

Modern televisions and computer monitors have screens with a liquid crystal display (LCD). The LCDs have millions of tiny dots known as pixels, each containing a red, green, and blue liquid crystal. Electricity passed through the crystals controls the amount of light, sharpening the images and making the colors more vibrant.

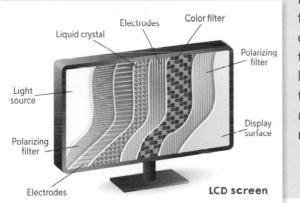

Electrodes
Color filter
Liquid crystal
Polarizing filter
Light source
Display surface
Polarizing filter
Electrodes

LCD screen

DOES A BATTERY PRODUCE ELECTRICITY?

No, it doesn't. A battery only stores energy in chemicals. When the battery is connected to a circuit, this chemical energy is converted to electrical energy.

Batteries

Rapid-FIRE ?

WHO INVENTED THE FIRST LIGHT BULB?

Thomas Edison, in January, 1879.

Thomas Edison

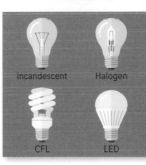

ARE LED LIGHTS EFFICIENT?

Yes, they use less energy than other bulbs.

Types of light bulbs

Incandescent   Halogen
CFL   LED

WHAT IS AN LED?

Light-emitting diode—a semiconductor that produces light when an electrical current is passed through it.

LED bulbs

WHAT IS RADIOACTIVITY?

When the nucleus of an atom becomes unstable and breaks down, it becomes radioactive, leaking radiation in the form of alpha, beta, and gamma rays. These high-energy rays can be dangerous, especially in large doses, causing burns and an increased risk of cancer.

Deserted radioactive zone, Chernobyl, Russia

Rapid-FIRE ?

WHY IS **FOOD GIVEN IONIZING RADIATION?**

To kill bacteria and other harmful substances; it does not make the food radioactive.

Eggs being cleaned by UV irradiation

WHO WERE THE "RADIUM GIRLS"?

In the 1910s young women in the US who painted watch dials with radium were called the "radium girls." Many were harmed by radium's radioactive properties.

The "radium girls" at work

WHAT IS A **BECQUEREL?**

It is the standard unit for measuring radioactivity.

IS **RADIATION VISIBLE?**

Radiation is basically energy shot out by atoms that are spinning at very high speeds. Most radiation is tiny bursts of "waves," such as X-rays, microwaves, radio waves, and light. Light is the only form of radiation we can see; all the rest are invisible. Radiation that comes in waves is called electromagnetic radiation because it is linked to electricity and magnetism.

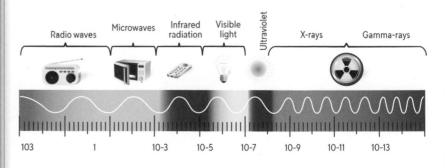

| Radio waves | Microwaves | Infrared radiation | Visible light | Ultraviolet | X-rays | Gamma-rays |

103   1   10-3   10-5   10-7   10-9   10-11   10-13

Electromagnetic spectrum

WHAT IS **NUCLEAR FUSION?**

The pushing together of atomic nuclei inside stars or in nuclear bombs starts a reaction where the nuclei combine to form different nuclei and subatomic particles. This process releases a great deal of energy.

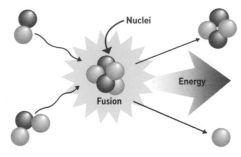

Nuclei

Energy

Fusion

Nuclear fusion

Big? **WHAT ARE RADIOISOTOPES?**

Microwave cooking

HOW DOES A **MICROWAVE WORK?**

Microwave ovens work by bombarding food with electromagnetic microwaves. The molecules of water in the food behave like magnets and are turned back and forth so quickly by electromagnetic vibrations that they heat up at great speed.

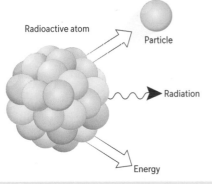

Radioactive atom

Particle

Radiation

Energy

Radiation release

Atoms of an element may exist in several different forms, or isotopes. Each form has a different number of neutrons in the nucleus; this is indicated by the name; for example, carbon-12 and carbon-14. The nuclei of some of these isotopes—the ones scientists call radioisotopes—are unstable and they decay (break up), releasing radiation.

WHAT IS A **HALF-LIFE?**

While it is not possible to predict when the nucleus of an atom will decay fully, scientists can predict how long it will take for the radioactivity of an element to decay to half of its original value—this is its half-life. As examples, francium-223 has a half-life of 22 minutes; uranium-238 has a half-life of 4.5 billion years. This concept can also be applied to other sciences. In medicine, for example, it is used to calculate how long a drug will take to be reduced to half its value in the body.

WHAT IS NUCLEAR POWER?

Though an atomic nucleus is tiny, the energy that binds it together is enormous. By harnessing this energy, nuclear power stations can generate huge amounts of power with just a few tons of nuclear fuel.

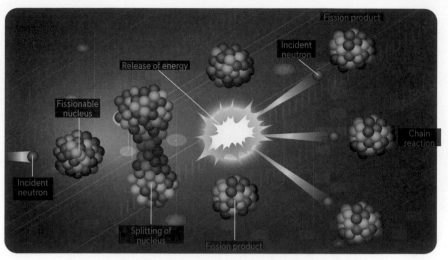

Nuclear fission releases tremendous amounts of energy that can be harnessed.

HOW MUCH ELECTRICITY IS MADE BY NUCLEAR POWER?

Nuclear power produces more than 11 percent of the world's electricity. Some people oppose any further increase because the highly radioactive fuel used is difficult to dispose of safely. The US, Russia, Canada, France, and Japan are the top producers of nuclear electricity.

Nuclear power station

Clean energy

Big?

WHAT ARE THE BENEFITS OF USING NUCLEAR POWER?

Nuclear power is a clean energy source. Unlike fossil fuels, it does not emit any poisonous gases—it does not load the air with pollutants that cause acid rain and smog. The fuel used for nuclear power is a million times more dense than other fuels, so a relatively tiny amount produces a huge amount of power. There are advanced power stations that can also operate on used fuels. One of the most efficient aspects of nuclear power is how little space it takes up in the land. A 1,000-megawatt power plant can be built on less than 2.5 square miles, while a solar power plant needs almost 75 times more land!

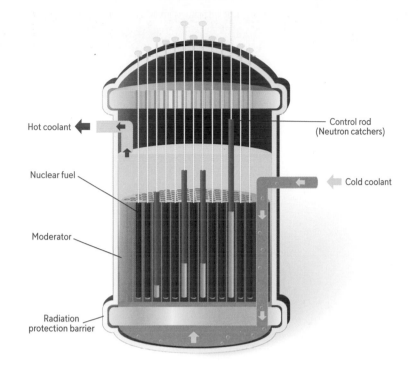

Hot coolant

Control rod
(Neutron catchers)

Nuclear fuel

Cold coolant

Moderator

Radiation
protection barrier

HOW DOES A NUCLEAR POWER STATION WORK?

In nuclear power stations, the nuclei of uranium atoms are split by firing tiny alpha particles at them, thereby releasing a huge amount of energy. This energy is used to heat water, which produces steam to drive the turbines, or wheels, that generate electricity.

Nuclear reactor

Atomic explosion

WHAT IS AN ATOMIC BOMB?

Used as a weapon, it is a powerful explosive device. Its power is the result of a sudden release of enormous amounts of energy created during nuclear fission: splitting of the nuclei of a heavy element, such as uranium.

HOW IS URANIUM PROCESSED FOR THE REACTOR?

Reactors use uranium, processed as uranium dioxide, which is formed into small ceramic pellets. These are sealed inside metallic tubes known as fuel rods. Depending on the power plant's size, these rods are assembled in hundreds and then immersed in water, which absorbs the heat and also controls the fission to sustain the chain reaction.

Uranium

WHEN WAS THE **FIRST NUCLEAR-POWER ELECTRICITY PRODUCED?**

In 1951. Three years later, in 1954, the first nuclear plant was set up in the USSR (now Russia).

The first four nuclear-lit bulbs

WHO **USED NUCLEAR POWERED SUBMARINES FIRST?**

The US Navy, in 1954: USS *Nautilus* was the first nuclear-powered submarine used.

Nuclear submarine

WHAT ARE THE **THREE KINDS OF REACTORS?**

Pressurized reactors, boiling water reactors, and gas-cooled reactors.

WHY IS LIGHT IMPORTANT?

Light is one form of electromagnetic radiation—the only form we can see. It is vital to us since without it, we couldn't see anything. Very few things emit their own light—the Sun does, and is the major source of light for Earth. It also provides warmth and energy and plants use its light for photosynthesis, a process that produces both oxygen and food and supports life on Earth.

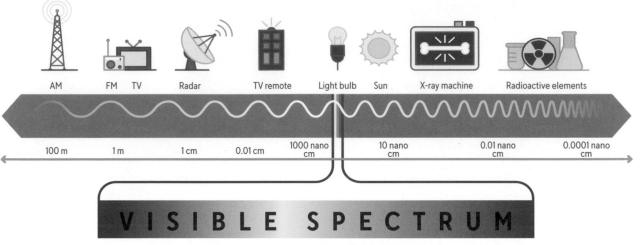

AM	FM TV	Radar	TV remote	Light bulb	Sun	X-ray machine	Radioactive elements

| 100 m | 1 m | 1 cm | 0.01 cm | 1000 nano cm | 10 nano cm | 0.01 nano cm | 0.0001 nano cm |

VISIBLE SPECTRUM

Light within the electromagnetic spectrum

WHAT'S THE FASTEST THING IN THE UNIVERSE?

Light—it travels at over 186,000 miles per second. This is the one speed in the Universe that is constant—always the same no matter how fast you are going when you measure it. Danish astronomer Ole Rømer first discovered the speed of light.

The Sun's rays

Rapid-FIRE ?

WHICH ARE THE LONGEST AND SHORTEST WAVELENGTHS?

The longest is red, while violet is the shortest.

380–450 nanometer	450–480 nanometer	480–510 nanometer	510–575 nanometer	575–585 nanometer	585–620 nanometer	620–780 nanometer

Comparing wavelengths of the visible spectrum

HOW DOES A PRISM WORK?

A prism is a transparent body with flat surfaces and sharp angles that breaks up white light into its different colors when it exits.

White light broken up as it passes through a prism

WHY IS THE SKY BLUE?

Molecules in the air scatter the particles of white light and more blue reaches our eyes than the other colors.

Seeing the blue in light

WHEN DOES THE SUN APPEAR RED?

The Sun appears red at sunrise and sunset, when it is low in the sky. At these times, sunlight reaches Earth only after passing at an angle through the dense lower layers of the atmosphere. Particles in the air absorb the shorter, bluer wavelengths of light or reflect them away from us, leaving just red to reach Earth and be seen.

Red sunset

WHAT ARE PHOTONS?

Photons are incredibly small particles of light and also tiny packets of energy. A single beam of light has billions of photons. Photons have no mass.

Light source

Beams made up of photons

Billions of photons make up the light that reaches your eyes

WHAT DOES "VIBGYOR" MEAN?

"VIBGYOR," or "ROYGBIV," is an abbreviation used for the order of the visible colors in white light. When white light refracts, it breaks up into seven different colors that can be seen in a fixed order: violet, indigo, blue, green, yellow, orange, and red, like in a rainbow.

A rainbow

Big ? WHAT IS WAVELENGTH?

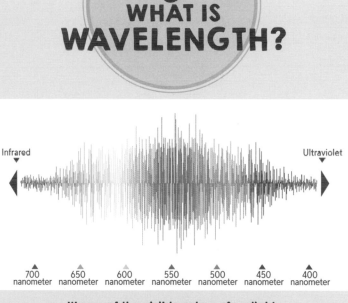

Infrared

Ultraviolet

| 700 nanometer | 650 nanometer | 600 nanometer | 550 nanometer | 500 nanometer | 450 nanometer | 400 nanometer |

Waves of the visible colors of sunlight

Light travels in waves. Wavelength is the distance between the top of one wave and the top of the next. The different colors of light have different wavelengths. We can see this when light refracts (bends) as it goes through a prism. Different colors emerge from a prism at different points, depending on how much they have been refracted, and the longer the wavelength of light, the more it is refracted. Wavelength is measured and denoted by a Greek word called *lambda*.

HOW DOES LIGHT WORK?

Light is a form of energy that is emitted, or radiated, by atoms. There are many sources of light, including the Sun, light bulbs, and flames. It is the light's ability to be reflected that allows us to see. The study of light, known as optics, describes how light is reflected, absorbed, or bent when it hits an object.

Reflections of light

HOW DO MIRRORS REFLECT IMAGES?

Most mirrors are backed with a shiny metal layer that perfectly reflects all the light that hits it, at exactly the same angle. The image that is created is not, in fact, back-to-front. Left is on the left, and right is on the right—which is the opposite of how we look to someone who is facing us.

Mirror reflection

Big?

WHAT IS THE DIFFERENCE BETWEEN REFLECTION AND REFRACTION?

When light strikes a semitransparent or nontransparent surface, it usually scatters in all directions. From shiny surfaces, however, and mirrors in particular, it bounces back in exactly the same pattern in which it hit the surface. This is called reflection. When light passes through something transparent, the rays go straight through or, if they are forced to slow down as they enter, they bend. The bending of light rays is called refraction.

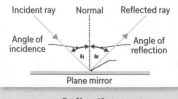

Reflection

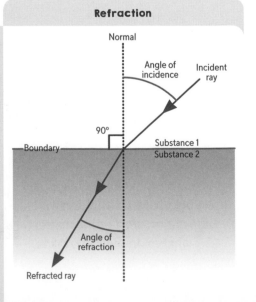

Refraction

WHY DOES LIGHT BEND?

When light rays strike a transparent material at an angle, they bend, or are refracted. Also, different materials let light waves through at different speeds. When light rays slow down, they bend.

The pencil appears crooked when it enters the water at an angle.

WHAT ARE TRANSPARENT, TRANSLUCENT, AND OPAQUE OBJECTS?

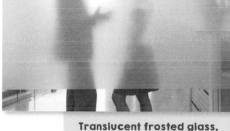

Translucent frosted glass, transparent at the bottom

Anything that lets light pass straight through, such as glass, is called transparent. If a surface breaks and jumbles up the particles of light as they pass through, as with frosted glass, it is translucent. If all the light bounces back, as it does with a wall, the object is termed opaque.

HOW DO FIBER-OPTIC CABLES WORK?

Inside a fiber-optic cable are bundles of glass fibers. Light rays zigzag along the inside of each fiber, reflecting first off one side, then off the other. This allows light to be transmitted with minimum distortion, no matter what route the cable takes.

Fiber-optic cables

Rapid-FIRE?

WHAT DO CONCAVE AND CONVEX LENSES DO?

Concave lenses curve outward like a dome, and they spread light out; convex lenses curve inward like a bowl and bring light rays together.

Convex lenses in spectacles

HOW DO BINOCULARS WORK?

The combination of lenses in binoculars gathers light rays to make things look closer and larger.

Binoculars

WHAT ARE THE PRIMARY COLORS IN LIGHT?

Red, green, and blue are the primary colors in light; the other colors are created when these three colors mix.

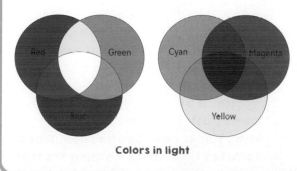

Colors in light

WHAT IS THE ELECTROMAGNETIC SPECTRUM?

Light is just a small part of the wide range of radiation emitted by atoms, and the only part humans can see. In addition to light, there are infrared rays (which are long waves), ultraviolet rays (which are short waves), radio waves, gamma rays, and others. The entire range of radiation is called the electromagnetic spectrum.

Radio | Microwave | Infrared | Visible light | Ultraviolet | X-rays | Gamma

UVA 400 380 365 | UVB 320 300 280 | UVC 254 200 180 nanometer

The electromagnetic spectrum

IS EXPOSURE TO ULTRAVIOLET LIGHT HARMFUL?

Ultraviolet light makes up only 5 percent of the Sun's electromagnetic radiation, but if all of it reached Earth, life on the planet would be severely affected. Fortunately, most of it is absorbed by the ozone layer. Though not lethal to humans, ultraviolet radiation can destroy organisms such as bacteria as well as individual tissue cells. The most often seen effect of exposure is sunburn—which can range from a mild redness to actual blistering and swelling of the skin. Long-term exposure can result in other skin problems, including cancer.

Big? WHAT ARE RADIO WAVES?

They are a kind of electromagnetic wave used mostly in communication technology. Italian inventor Guglielmo Marconi first sent radio signals in 1895, over a distance of 5,200 ft. In 1901 he sent a radio message across the Atlantic Ocean. Today, these waves are used for television broadcasts and in cell phones. These devices receive radio waves of various frequencies and convert them to other forms of signals such as sound. Radio frequency, though very important, is a small part of the electromagnetic spectrum. According to NASA, radio waves have the longest wavelength in the electromagnetic spectrum.

A communications tower

HOW DO **TV SIGNALS TRAVEL?**

TV signals travel in one of three ways. Terrestrial broadcasts are beamed out from transmitters as radio waves to be picked up by TV aerials. Satellite broadcasts are sent up to satellites as microwaves, then sent back to Earth to be picked up by satellite dishes. Cable broadcasts travel as electrical or light signals along underground cables, straight to the TV set.

Satellite dish and TV aerial

WHAT ARE MICROWAVES USED FOR BESIDES COOKING?

They are also used in radars for predicting weather.

A weather satellite

WHO ESTABLISHED THE LAWS OF ELECTROSTATIC AND MAGNETISM?

Charles Coulomb, a French physicist, in 1785.

Charles Coulomb

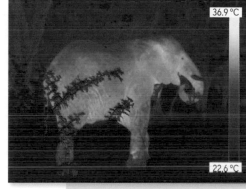
Infrared image of an African elephant

36.9 °C
22.6 °C

IS IT POSSIBLE TO **SEE INFRARED RAYS?**

Infrared is light of wavelengths too long for the human eye to register. Infrared light, however, is experienced as warmth, and anything that gives off heat also gives off infrared waves. Night vision cameras use these waves to monitor movement of animals and humans. Some animals, such as mosquitoes, some nocturnal species of bats, and snakes use these waves of the electromagnetic spectrum to "see" and hunt.

DO **GAMMA RAYS HAVE ANY MEDICAL USE?**

Yes, they are often used to treat cancer.

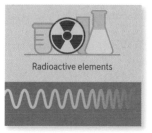
Radioactive elements

Gamma rays

WHAT ARE **NEAR-INFRARED WAVES USED FOR?**

They are used in various remote controls.

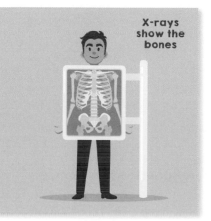
X-rays show the bones

HOW ARE **X-RAYS USEFUL?**

X-ray wavelengths are so short that for scientists they cross over to being more like particles than waves. As they can go through soft tissue in the human body, doctors use them to check for broken or deformed bones. But too much exposure to X-rays is also harmful.

WHAT IS SOUND?

Sounds are vibrations that can be heard. Sometimes you can see the vibration that creates the sound—when you pluck an elastic band, for instance. When you clap your hands, however, you don't see the vibrations, though you can hear the sound. The movement of your hands causes molecules in the air to move and set off a wave of sound that is transmitted through the air to your ears.

Creating waves that can be heard

Big ? WHY DOES SOUND ECHO?

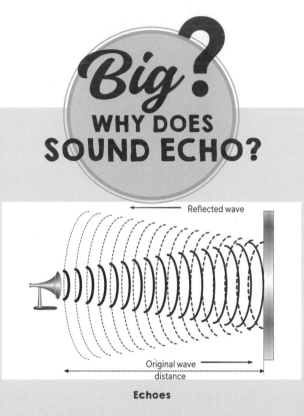

Reflected wave

Original wave
distance

Echoes

An echo is a sound that has bounced back to its source. We don't often hear echoes, because sound waves travel through gases, liquids, and solids. They only bounce off smooth, hard, wall-like surfaces in confined spaces. Because we hear echoes only when the sound bounces back at least 0.1 seconds after it is made, even in a confined space, the wall must be at least 56 ft away. This is why echoes can be heard only in large, empty halls. A good example of an echo is when you shout in a tunnel and the sound waves rebound off the walls around.

WHAT IS THE SPEED OF SOUND?

The speed of sound is generally measured as it travels through air at sea level at 59 °F. In these conditions its speed is about 761.2 miles per hour. But sound travels through all substances—solid, liquid, and gas, and at all temperatures—and its speed varies. For instance, it travels faster through solids and on a hot day.

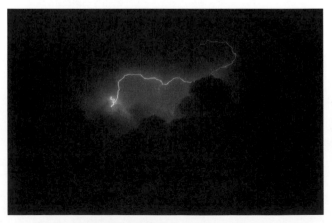

Sound is slower than light, which is why thunder is heard after lightning is seen.

DOES SOUND HAVE DIFFERENT FREQUENCIES?

The frequency with which sound waves are created makes sounds different from each other. If the sound waves follow after each other closely, they are high frequency and make a high-pitched sound, like a whistle. If the waves are far apart, they are low frequency and make a low sound, like a drum.

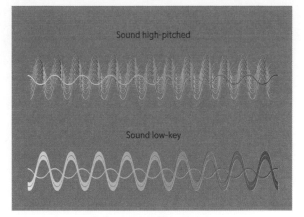

Sound high-pitched

Sound low-key

High and low frequencies

WHAT DETERMINES THE VOLUME OF SOUND?

Wave length

Amplitude

The loudness of a sound is called its volume, or amplitude. This is the amount of pressure exerted by the source of the sound on air molecules. The higher the pressure, the harder the molecules will collide, the farther they will travel, and the louder the sound will be.

Sound waves and volume

CAN SOUND TRAVEL IN A VACUUM?

No, sound travels by setting off a wave of vibrating molecules. The molecules in solids are closely packed, which allows sound to travel faster. In a vacuum, where there is nothing to vibrate, sound cannot travel. There is always complete silence.

Rapid-FIRE ?

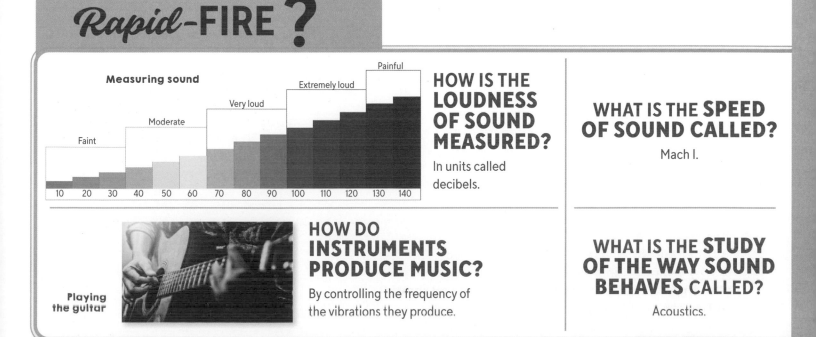

Measuring sound

Painful

Extremely loud

Very loud

Moderate

Faint

10 20 30 40 50 60 70 80 90 100 110 120 130 140

HOW IS THE LOUDNESS OF SOUND MEASURED?

In units called decibels.

WHAT IS THE SPEED OF SOUND CALLED?

Mach I.

Playing the guitar

HOW DO INSTRUMENTS PRODUCE MUSIC?

By controlling the frequency of the vibrations they produce.

WHAT IS THE STUDY OF THE WAY SOUND BEHAVES CALLED?

Acoustics.

HOW DO SOUND WAVES WORK?

Sound waves don't go up and down. They move by alternately stretching and squeezing. When a sound is made, air molecules near the sound are pushed together. They, in turn, knock into the molecules next to them, and then are pulled back into place by the molecules behind.

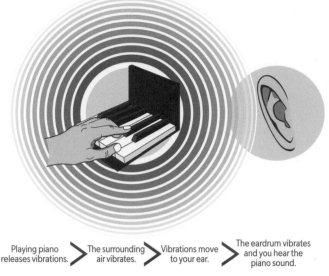

Playing piano releases vibrations. > The surrounding air vibrates. > Vibrations move to your ear. > The eardrum vibrates and you hear the piano sound.

Sound waves push outward as they travel.

HOW DOES AN AIRPLANE BREAK THE SOUND BARRIER?

As an airplane flies, not only does it squash the air in front, it also pushes up against the sound waves it is creating. If it reaches a speed faster than that of the sound waves, it can break through them, generating a shock wave that sounds like a loud explosive sound called a sonic boom.

Breaking the sound barrier

Big ? CAN SOUND TRAVEL THROUGH SOLIDS AND LIQUIDS?

It is the vibration of molecules that causes sound to travel. Therefore, any substance that has a molecular structure will conduct sound. Sound travels through solids and liquids in the same way as it does through the air. In fact, because molecules of liquids are more closely packed than those of air, sound travels better through most liquids than it does through air. The best conductors of sounds, those that transmit sound faster and farther, are rigid solids such as iron and steel. Some solids, such as rubber, cork, and cloth, are weak sound conductors. They do not pass on vibrations but absorb them and are used to create soundproof environments.

Sound waves in air, water, and metal

Pressure   f=100 hz   Air
Wavelength = 11.28 ft

Pressure   Water
Wavelength = 48 ft

Pressure   Steel
Wavelength = 168.47 ft

WHY DOES THE SOUND OF A CAR'S ENGINE DROP IN PITCH AS IT ZOOMS AWAY?

It happens because the sound waves are stretched out behind it. This is called the Doppler effect, and it was first established in 1842 by Christian Doppler, an Austrian scientist. It is used to measure the speed at which a star recedes or approaches Earth.

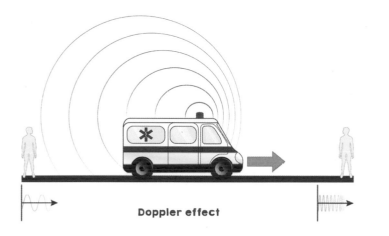

Doppler effect

WHAT IS **RESONANCE?**

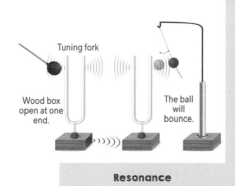

Tuning fork

Wood box open at one end.

The ball will bounce.

Resonance

When an object vibrates freely, it will always do so at its natural frequency. If you jog it, you can make it vibrate faster or slower. But, if you jog it at just the same rate as its natural frequency, it will vibrate in sympathy and the vibrations become stronger. This is called resonance.

CAN WE **HEAR A BAT'S ECHOLOCATION CALL?**

No. Bats call at a frequency that is too high for the human ear to hear. Some can be heard, but this is very rare.

Bat in flight

WHAT IS THE **HIGHEST FREQUENCY HUMANS CAN HEAR?**

20,000 Hz (frequency is measured in Hertz).

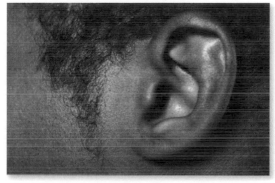

The outer ear

WHAT DOES A **LARGE SOUND WAVE MEAN?**

The larger the wave, the louder the sound.

HOW DO **BATS LOCATE THEIR FOOD?**

Most bats locate their prey using echolocation. They send out very high-pitched calls, and use the echoes to find and identify objects. Echolocation is also used for navigating in complete darkness.

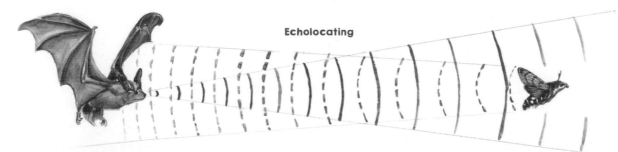

Echolocating

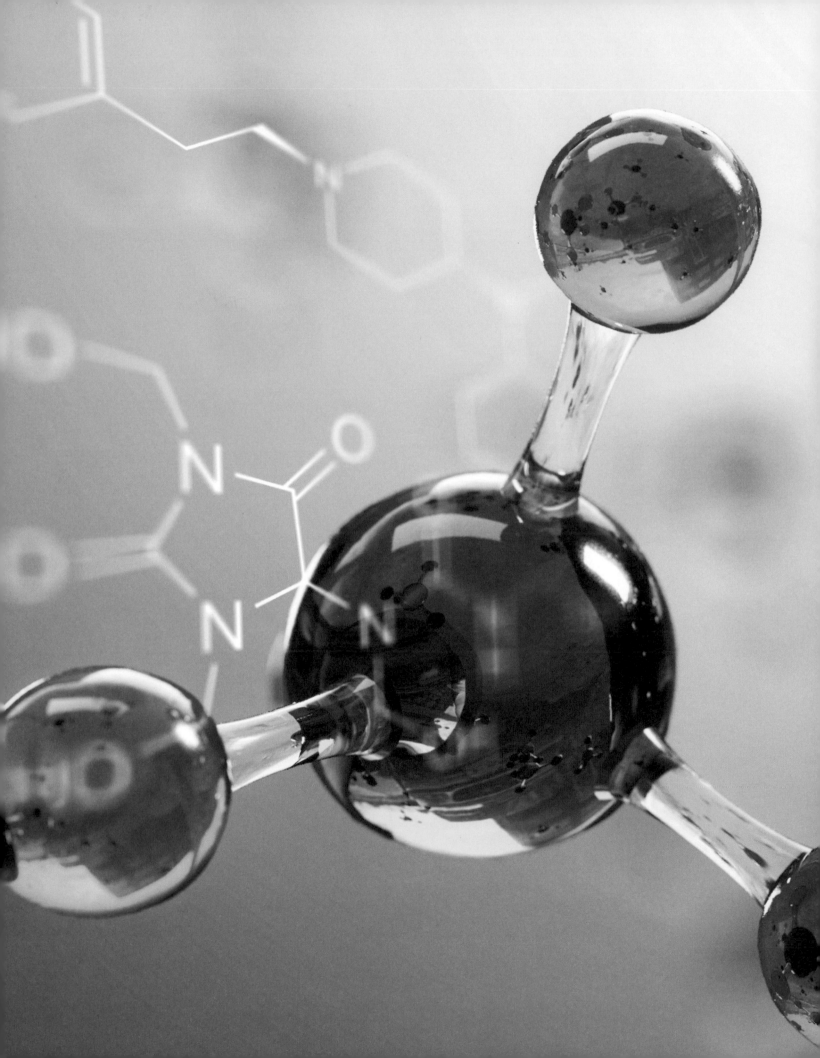

ELEMENTS AND COMPOUNDS

6
C
4
2
Carbon
12,011

The element carbon

WHAT IS AN ELEMENT?

An element is a pure substance that is made of only one type of atom. These atoms have their own unique character and cannot be split into other substances, which means an element cannot be reduced to anything simpler. Everything in the Universe is made up of elements.

WHICH ELEMENT IS THE LIGHTEST?

Hydrogen is the lightest element. It has only one proton in its nucleus and, thus, has an atomic mass of one. It is also the most common element in the Universe.

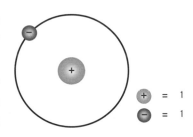

+ = 1
− = 1

Hydrogen atom

Big?
HOW ARE ELEMENTS IDENTIFIED?

In each atom of each element is a unique number of protons and electrons. In the element's standard state, these protons and electrons are equal in number. For instance, a hydrogen atom has one proton and one electron. The number of protons and electrons in the atom of each element is what identifies it, and makes it different from other elements. The fact that nitrogen has seven protons while carbon has six is what makes them completely different elements.

Nitrogen symbol

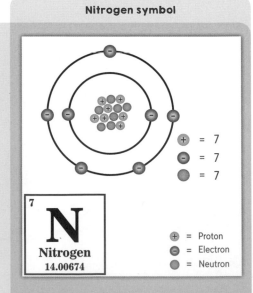

+ = 7
− = 7
● = 7

7
N
Nitrogen
14.00674

+ = Proton
− = Electron
● = Neutron

WHAT IS **ATOMIC MASS?**

Atomic mass is the "weight" of one whole atom, including both protons and electrons, of any substance, which is of course very tiny! The first scientists to determine atomic mass were John Dalton and Thomas Thomson.

John Dalton　　**Thomas Thomson**

WHAT ARE **METALS?**

Metals are hard, dense, shiny solids. They are good conductors of heat and electricity because they are electropositive, which means their electrons can easily become "free." Most metals can be beaten into sheets and can be made into wire.

Metal wire

WHAT IS AN **ATOMIC NUMBER?**

The number of protons present in an atom's nucleus is balanced by the number of electrons that revolve around the nucleus. It is the number of protons that gives an element its atomic number. Because hydrogen has just a single proton, it has an atomic number of one.

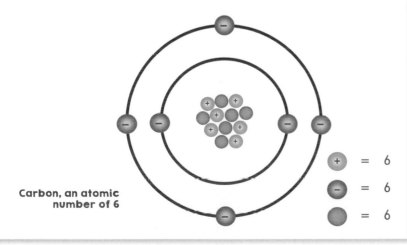

Carbon, an atomic number of 6

+ = 6
− = 6
● = 6

Rapid-FIRE **?**

WHICH **ELEMENT IS COMMON IN THE UNIVERSE BUT RARE ON EARTH?**

The gas, helium.

Filling a balloon with helium gas

HOW MANY **ELEMENTS** ARE THERE?

Currently, there are 118 known elements.

ARE THE **ELEMENTS DIFFERENT ON EARTH AND MARS?**

No, they are exactly the same.

WHAT IS AN **ATOMIC SYMBOL?**

Each element has a short name made up of one or two letters of the English alphabet, which is called its symbol. If it has two letters, then the first letter is written in capitals and the second in small letters. Carbon is written as C, hydrogen as H, copper as Cu, and oxygen as O.

WHAT IS THE **PERIODIC TABLE?**

All chemical elements are displayed in a systematic order in a chart called the periodic table.

Group → Period ↓	1 IA	2 IIA	3 IIIB	4 IVB	5 VB	6 VIB	7 VIIB	8 VIIIB	9 VIIIB	10 VIIIB	11 IB	12 IIB	13 IIIA	14 IVA	15 VA	16 VIA	17 VIIA	18 VIIIA
1	1 H Hydrogen 1.00794																	2 He Helium 4.002602
2	3 Li Lithium 6.941	4 Be Beryllium 9.012182											5 B Boron 10.811	6 C Carbon 12.0107	7 N Nitrogen 14.0067	8 O Oxygen 15.9994	9 F Fluorine 18.9984032	10 Ne Neon 20.1797
3	11 Na Sodium 22.98976928	12 Mg Magnesium 24.305											13 Al Aluminium 26.9815386	14 Si Silicon 28.0855	15 P Phosphorus 30.973762	16 S Sulfur 32.065	17 Cl Chlorine 35.453	18 Ar Argon 39.948
4	19 K Potassium 39.0983	20 Ca Calcium 40.078	21 Sc Scandium 44.9559	22 Ti Titanium 47.867	23 V Vanadium 50.9415	24 Cr Chromium 51.9961	25 Mn Manganese 54.938045	26 Fe Iron 55.845	27 Co Cobalt 58.933195	28 Ni Nickel 58.6934	29 Cu Copper 63.546	30 Zn Zinc 65.38	31 Ga Gallium 69.729	32 Ge Germanium 72.64	33 As Arsenic 74.9216	34 Se Selenium 78.96	35 Br Bromine 79.904	36 Kr Krypton 83.798
5	37 Rb Rubidium 85.4678	38 Sr Strontium 87.62	39 Y Yttrium 88.90585	40 Zr Zirconium 91.224	41 Nb Niobium 92.9063	42 Mo Molybdenum 95.96	43 Tc Technetium [98]	44 Ru Ruthenium 101.07	45 Rh Rhodium 102.9055	46 Pd Palladium 106.42	47 Ag Silver 107.8682	48 Cd Cadmium 112.411	49 In Indium 114.818	50 Sn Tin 118.71	51 Sb Antimony 121.76	52 Te Tellurium 127.6	53 I Iodine 126.90447	54 Xe Xenon 131.293
6	55 Cs Caesium 132.9054519	56 Ba Barium 137.327	57-71 Lanthanoids	72 Hf Hafnium 178.49	73 Ta Tantalum 180.94788	74 W Tungsten 183.84	75 Re Rhenium 186.207	76 Os Osmium 190.23	77 Ir Iridium 192.217	78 Pt Platinum 195.084	79 Au Gold 196.966569	80 Hg Mercury 200.59	81 Tl Thallium 204.3833	82 Pb Lead 207.2	83 Bi Bismuth 208.9804	84 Po Polonium [209]	85 At Astatine [222]	86 Rn Radon [222]
7	87 Fr Francium [223]	88 Ra Radium [226]	89-103 Actinoids	104 Rf Rutherfordium [267]	105 Db Dubnium [268]	106 Sg Seaborgium [271]	107 Bh Bohrium [272]	108 Hs Hassium [270]	109 Mt Meitnerium [276]	110 Ds Darmstadtium [281]	111 Rg Roentgenium [280]	112 Cn Copernicium [285]	113 Uut Ununtrium [286]	114 Fl Flerovium [289]	115 Uup Ununpentium [288]	116 Lv Livermorium [293]	117 Uus Ununseptium [294]	118 Uuo Ununoctium [294]

Atomic number → | 1 | 1 ← Electrons per shell
H ← Symbol
Hydrogen ← Name
1.00794 ← Atomic weight

Lanthanoids →	57 La Lanthanum 138.90547	58 Ce Cerium 140.116	59 Pr Praseodymium 140.90765	60 Nd Neodymium 144.242	61 Pm Promethium [145]	62 Sm Samarium 150.36	63 Eu Europium 151.964	64 Gd Gadolinium 157.25	65 Tb Terbium 158.9253	66 Dy Dysprosium 162.5	67 Ho Holmium 164.93032	68 Er Erbium 167.259	69 Tm Thulium 168.93421	70 Yb Ytterbium 173.054	71 Lu Lutetium 174.9668
Actinoids →	89 Ac Actinium [227]	90 Th Thorium 232.03806	91 Pa Protactinium 231.03588	92 U Uranium 238.02891	93 Np Neptunium [237]	94 Pu Plutonium [244]	95 Am Americium [243]	96 Cm Curium [247]	97 Bk Berkelium [247]	98 Cf Californium [251]	99 Es Einsteinium [252]	100 Fm Fermium [257]	101 Md Mendelevium [258]	102 No Nobelium [262]	103 Lr Lawrencium [262]

Legend: Post-transition metals | Transition metals | Lanthanide | Alkaline earth metals | Metalloids | Alkali metals | Other nonmetals | Halogens | Actinide | Noble gases | Radioactive element | Synthetic element | H Gas | Hg Liquid | Li Solid

Periodic table of the elements

Big? HOW IS THE PERIODIC TABLE ORGANIZED?

The periodic table organizes elements in the order of their atomic numbers, starting with hydrogen, which has an atomic number of one. It is laid out in 18 columns called "groups" and seven rows called "periods." Each group is formed of elements that have a similar atomic structure. Periods are made up of elements that have similar chemical properties such as how volatile they are or how well they conduct heat. Metals are given on the left side and nonmetals on the right side of the periods.

Chemical symbols

WHAT ARE **LANTHANIDES?**

Lanthanides are a collection of 15 elements placed one row above the bottom of the table. They have two or three electrons in their outer shells and are all shiny, silvery metals that often occur naturally together.

Lanthanides

WHAT IS **GROUP 0?**

Group 18 on the far right is also called group 0. It is made up of what are called the noble gases. The outer shells of the atoms of these gases have as many electrons as can be accommodated, so they do not react with other elements. This is why they are sometimes also called "inert."

Krypton

[Ar]$3d^{10}4s^24p^6$

83,798

36

Kr

2
8
18
8

Krypton, a noble gas

WHICH ARE THE **MOST COMMON ELEMENTS IN EARTH'S CRUST?**

The composition of Earth's crust is very different from that of other planets in the Universe. Oxygen, at nearly 46 percent, is the most available element. Silicon is second at just over 27 percent, followed by aluminium, iron, calcium, sodium, potassium, and magnesium. These eight elements make up more than 98 percent of the crust.

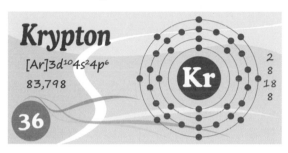

%	%	%	%
▉ O2	▉ Fe	▉ K	▉ Ti
▉ Si	▉ Ca	▉ Mg	▉ C
▉ Al	▉ Na	▉ H	▉ Other elements

Chemical composition of Earth's crust

WHAT ARE **POOR METALS?**

These are located in columns 13 to 15 and have a low melting point.

The poor metals

WHICH ARE THE **TRANSITION METALS?**

Metals in the middle of the periodic table, such as gold and silver.

The transition metals

HOW **MANY NONMETAL ELEMENTS ARE THERE?**

A total of 21.

HOW ARE **REACTIVE AND STABLE ELEMENTS DIVIDED IN THE TABLE?**

Each period starts on the left with a highly reactive "alkali metal," which has one electron in its outer shell. It ends on the right with a stable "noble gas," such as argon, krypton, or xenon, which has eight electrons in its outer shell.

From stable elements (left) to unstable elements (right)

WHAT IS THE DIFFERENCE BETWEEN SOLIDS AND LIQUIDS?

A solid is a substance that has a definite shape and volume. The molecules of a solid are firmly locked together in a bond that has a regular structure. A liquid is a fluid substance that has no defined shape but takes the shape of whatever contains it. Its molecules are not as firmly bonded as those of solids.

Molecules of a solid (left) and a liquid (right)

WHICH SUBSTANCE HAS THE LOWEST FREEZING POINT?

At -452 °F, helium has the lowest freezing point of all substances. This is less than four degrees above what is called absolute zero, -459.67 °F, the point at which no heat energy remains in a substance.

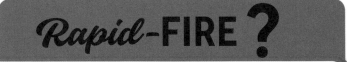

Rapid-FIRE ?

Dewdrops

WHAT IS DEW?

Water in the air that condenses and becomes liquid from gas.

Water gushing from a burst pipe

WHY DO WATER PIPES BURST DURING A WINTER FREEZE?

When water freezes, it expands, and cannot fit in the pipes any more.

Mercury

WHICH METAL IS THE LAST TO FREEZE?

Mercury has the lowest freezing point of any metal: -37.9 °F.

WHEN DO **SOLIDS MELT?**

When a solid is heated to a temperature that causes its molecules to loosen their bonds and become more fluid, it changes into liquid. The point at which the substance starts flowing is called its melting point, and it varies depending on the strength of the bond between molecules.

Ice melts to water.

WHAT MAKES **LIQUIDS FREEZE?**

When the temperature drops, the molecules of a liquid pack more and more closely together. There comes a point when they are so tightly packed that they are no longer fluid. This is when the liquid turns into a solid—it is called the freezing point.

Frozen water—ice

WHAT HAPPENS WHEN A **LIQUID BOILS?**

Water boiling

As the temperature of a liquid reaches boiling point, the bond between molecules weakens until it breaks down entirely, and molecules move away from each other. These "loose" molecules start rising to the surface and then escaping in the form of gas or steam until, gradually, all the liquid "evaporates" or turns into gas.

Big?
WHAT MAKES A **SOLID STRONG?**

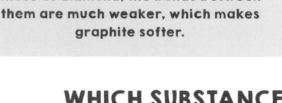
Graphite   Diamond

Molecules of graphite and diamond

The strength of a solid depends upon how firmly its molecules are bonded together. Diamond is the hardest solid of all because all its molecules are tightly bonded to make an incredibly strong structure. Though the molecules of graphite are similar to those of diamond, the bonds between them are much weaker, which makes graphite softer.

WHICH SUBSTANCE HAS THE **HIGHEST MELTING POINT?**

Carbon has the highest melting point of all substances. It melts at 6,917 °F. Tungsten, which melts at 6,177 °F, has the highest melting point among metals.

Light bulbs use tungsten filaments

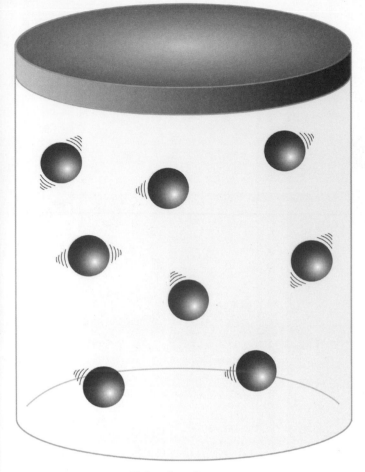

Molecules of gas

WHAT IS A GAS?

Gas is a state in which matter has no fixed shape or volume. The molecules inside gases constantly move at a speed that breaks the bonds that would otherwise hold them together. Gases can therefore expand and contract to fill any shape or size of container. Matter occupies more space as a gas than it would as a liquid or solid.

IS AIR MADE UP OF A SINGLE GAS?

No, air is a mixture of many gases and tiny particles. It contains 78 percent nitrogen and 21 percent oxygen, with traces of argon, carbon dioxide, helium, neon, krypton, xenon, and radon. It also carries dust, pollen, and water vapor.

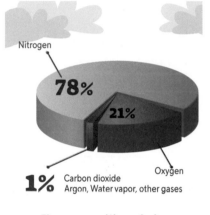

Nitrogen

78%

21%

Oxygen

1% Carbon dioxide
Argon, Water vapor, other gases

The composition of air

Big?
WHAT IS AIR PRESSURE?

Pressure is the amount of force that is applied to a substance. A very strong force creates high pressure, and a weak force creates low pressure. Air pressure is increased when the moving molecules of air push against an area. If air is squeezed into half the space without any change in its temperature, air pressure will double. If the temperature is raised, the pressure will increase as the heated air expands.

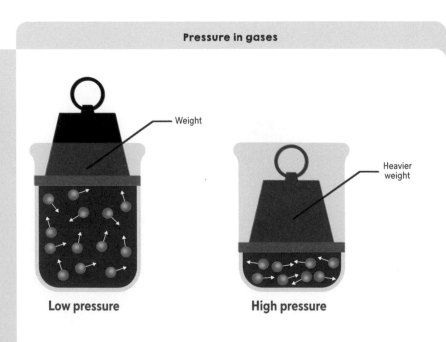

Pressure in gases

Weight

Heavier weight

Low pressure

High pressure

WHAT IS **FIRE?**

Fire is heat and light that is produced by a chemical reaction. It is created when molecules of certain substances are heated enough to break them apart. When this happens, the freed molecules combine with oxygen in the air to produce light and heat in the form of a flame. They also produce water and carbon dioxide.

WHY DOES A **HELIUM BALLOON RISE UP IN THE AIR?**

When a balloon made of latex or rubber is filled with helium gas, the combined weight of the balloon and the helium inside it is still lighter than air. Air pressure pushes and lifts the balloon upward.

Floating balloons

WHAT IS **PLASMA?**

Plasma is a state in which a gas becomes so hot that its atoms and molecules collide and electrons are ripped free. This is what happens inside the Sun and other stars when gases are heated by nuclear fusion. Plasma is also created during lightning.

The Sun

WHAT ARE **CLOUDS?**

As the Sun's rays heat the air, it rises; as it rises, the warm air cools down and the water vapor that it contains starts to become liquid and form droplets of water. These water droplets form clouds.

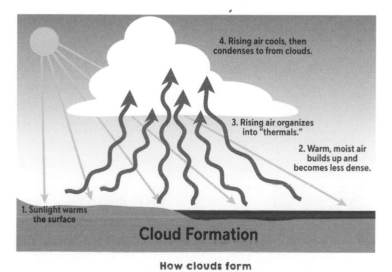

4. Rising air cools, then condenses to from clouds.

3. Rising air organizes into "thermals."

2. Warm, moist air builds up and becomes less dense.

1. Sunlight warms the surface

Cloud Formation

How clouds form

Rapid-FIRE **?**

IS **PLASMA THE MOST ABUNDANT STATE OF MATTER?**

Yes, the Universe is full of stars that are almost entirely plasma.

Stars

WHAT IS A **BAROMETER?**

An instrument that is used to measure air pressure.

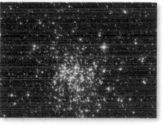

Barometer

WHICH GAS IS USED IN **HIGH-SPEED PHOTOGRAPHY?**

Krypton.

CAN GAS BE TURNED INTO **LIQUID BY APPLYING PRESSURE?**

Yes, it can.

WHAT IS A SOLUTION?

Substances do not always exist alone. They may also dissolve in, or mix with, other substances without becoming joined chemically. When a substance in a limited proportion becomes dissolved in a liquid or a gas, it forms a solution. Particles in a solution are always distributed evenly. For example, sugar mixed with water and fresh lemon juice forms a solution.

A solution

Rapid-FIRE **?**

IS SEAWATER A SOLUTION?

Yes, it is a solution of water and various kinds of salt.

Seawater

WHAT IS MEANT BY "MISCIBLE"?

When two liquids mix well to form a solution, they are called miscible.

WILL A SOLUTE SEPARATE FROM THE SOLVENT OVER A PERIOD OF TIME?

Never. Under normal circumstances, a solute will always remain dissolved.

HOW DO SUBSTANCES DISSOLVE?

For a substance to dissolve, its molecules have to be surrounded by the molecules of the solvent and spread evenly within it. This process, which interferes with the bonds between the molecules of both solute and solvent, also produces energy.

  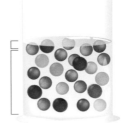

Solid   Liquid   Solution

Molecules in a solution

WHAT IS A **MIXTURE?**

Mixtures may contain several substances mixed, but not chemically joined, and they can be separated again with the right techniques. Unlike in solutions, the substances in mixtures may not be completely dissolved or uniformly distributed, and there is no fixed limit to each substance. Two very different examples of mixtures are Earth's atmosphere, with all its gases and particles, and mixed-grain flour.

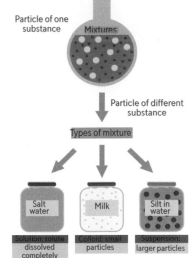

Mixtures can be of different consistencies

WHEN DOES A **SOLUTION REACH SATURATION?**

As a substance continues to dissolve in a liquid, there comes a point when the liquid cannot take any more and it stops dissolving the substance. This is the saturation point. Since liquids expand when they are heated, the saturation point varies with temperature.

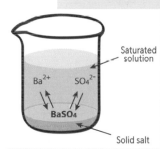

Saturated solution

WHAT IS THE DIFFERENCE BETWEEN **SOLUTE AND SOLVENT?**

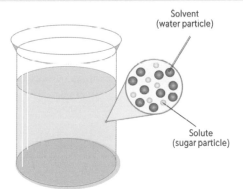

WHAT IS AN **ION?**

An ion is an atom that has either lost one or more electrons, leaving it positively charged, or has gained a few electrons making it negatively charged. Ions usually form when substances dissolve in a liquid. For example, when sodium chloride (common salt) dissolves in hydrogen oxide (water), the positive sodium attracts the negative oxygen, while the negative chloride attracts the positive hydrogen ions.

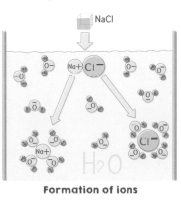

Formation of ions

Solution of water and sugar

A solution has two parts—the substance that dissolves, which is the solute, and the substance in which it dissolves, called the solvent. The amount of solvent is always greater than the amount of the solute. The solute can be either solid, liquid, or gas, but the solvent is usually liquid (though in some cases it could be a gas). The boiling point of the solute is always higher than that of the solvent. Water is referred to as a "universal solvent" because most substances dissolve in water, but there is no universal solute.

WHAT IS A CHEMICAL COMPOUND?

NO₂
Nitrogen dioxide

H₂O
Water

Elements do not always exist alone—they may dissolve in, or mix with, other elements. It is only when elements react chemically with each other to make a bond, however, that they form a compound. So, when table salt dissolves in water, it does not form a compound, but when sodium and chlorine combine, they make a compound called sodium chloride, or table salt.

NO
Nitrogen oxide

CO₂
Carbon dioxide

C
Carbon

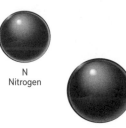

Elements combine to form compounds.

N
Nitrogen

H
Hydrogen

O₂
Oxygen

Big? HOW IS A CHEMICAL COMPOUND FORMED?

A molecule of glucose compound (C₆H₁₂O₆)

When two or more elements join together, they make a compound. Every molecule in a compound has the same combination of atoms of different elements, which are chemically bonded in the same way. The chemical formula of a compound defines how many atoms of each element make a molecule. Thus, a molecule of glucose compound has six atoms of carbon, 12 atoms of hydrogen, and six atoms of oxygen—its chemical formula is written as C₆H₁₂O₆. There are three types of bonds: ionic, covalent, and metallic. Each combines elements in a different way.

WHAT IS A METALLIC BOND?

In a metallic bond, a large number of electrons are shared between positively charged ions. They act as glue and give the substance a structure.

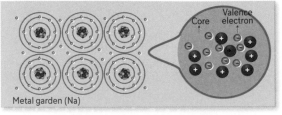

Core
Valence electron

Metal garden (Na)

How a metallic bond works

HOW DOES A COVALENT BOND WORK?

Stable atoms have a full set of eight electrons in their outer shells. Those that have too many or too few can get a full set by sharing electrons with other atoms. When atoms share electrons, they form a covalent bond. In water, two hydrogen atoms share electrons with one atom of oxygen.

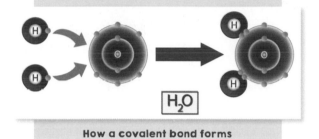

H_2O

How a covalent bond forms

| Water molecule H_2O | Hydrochloric acid molecule HCl | Hydrogen iodide molecule HI | Formaldehyde molecule CH_2O | Ammonia molecule NH_3 |

Polar molecules

WHY IS **WATER MADE UP OF POLAR MOLECULES?**

Water molecules are special. When sharing electrons with an atom of oxygen, the electrons of each hydrogen atom are pulled to the side closest to the oxygen atom. This exposes the positively charged nucleus by leaving the far side "bare." In this position water molecules have both a positive and a negative end, which is why they are known as polar molecules.

WHAT IS AN **IONIC BOND?**

Ionic bonds form when atoms with just a few electrons in their outer shells donate them to atoms with a few missing from theirs. When this happens, the atom losing electrons becomes positively charged, while the other is negatively charged. The atoms stick together because of electrical attraction.

Formation of an ionic bond

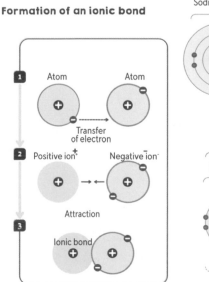

1 Atom — Atom
Transfer of electron

2 Positive ion⁺ — Negative ion⁻
Attraction

3 Ionic bond

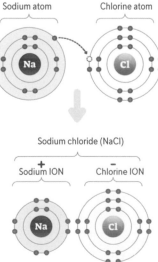

Sodium atom — Chlorine atom

Sodium chloride (NaCl)

⁺ Sodium ION — ⁻ Chlorine ION

Ionic bond

Rapid-FIRE **?**

WHAT IS **DNA?**

Deoxyribonucleic acid—the chemical compound in our bodies that carries genetic information.

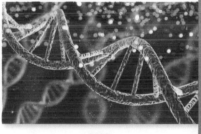

DNA

WHAT IS AN **ORGANIC COMPOUND MADE UP OF?**

Most organic compounds are carbon compounds.

WHICH COMPOUND HAS A SIX-SIDED STRUCTURE?

Benzene, which is used to make plastics, pesticides, and other industrial goods.

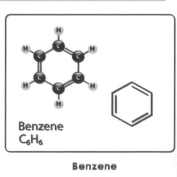

Benzene C_6H_6

Benzene

WHAT IS A CHEMICAL FORMULA?

A chemical formula is a short description of an atom, an ion, or a molecule. Generally, the initial letter of the name identifies the atom or ion and a number indicates how many atoms are involved. So, the formula for water is H_2O, meaning that each molecule is made up of two hydrogen atoms and one oxygen atom.

Chemical reaction

WHAT IS AN ENDOTHERMIC REACTION?

This happens when a chemical reaction absorbs energy, resulting in a cooling effect on the immediate surroundings. For example, when cooking food, the heat generated is absorbed by the ingredients that are in the food, and in photosynthesis, plants absorb energy from the Sun and cool the surroundings.

Endothermic reaction

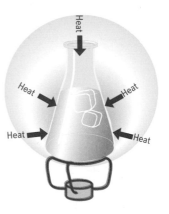

WHAT ARE THE DIFFERENT KINDS OF CHEMICAL REACTIONS?

There are five basic types. A combination reaction occurs when two or more substances combine to form a single new substance, such as chlorine reacting with sodium to form common salt. In a decomposition reaction, heat makes a complex compound break down into simpler substances. A single-replacement reaction involves one element replacing a similar element in a compound. A double-replacement reaction takes place when the positive and negative ions of two ionic compounds exchange places to form two new compounds. Lastly, in a combustion reaction, a substance reacts with oxygen and a tremendous amount of energy is released.

Chemical reactions

Single-displacement reaction

Double-displacement reaction

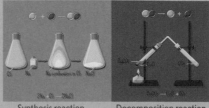

Synthesis reaction

Decomposition reaction

Combustion reaction

WHAT IS AN EXOTHERMIC REACTION?

A chemical reaction that creates more energy than is needed to cause the reaction is an exothermic reaction. In it, energy is released into the environment in the form of heat. The burning of wood is one example.

Exothermic reaction

HOW DO BATTERIES WORK?

Batteries generate an electric current from the reaction between two chemicals. One forms a positive electrode, which conducts electricity, while the other is negative. The reaction builds up an excess number of electrons on the negative electrode, which produces a current.

Switch

Battery

+

−

Light bulb

Wire

Battery power

Rapid-FIRE?

DOES EATING CANDY CREATE CHEMICAL REACTIONS IN OUR MOUTH?

Yes, the sugar in candy reacts with bacteria and produces acid.

Eating a sweet lollipop

WHAT CAUSES BREAD TO RISE?

The chemical reaction between yeast and sugar, when the dough is heated.

Bread dough rising

WHAT IS ELECTROLYSIS?

The process of breaking down compounds by passing an electric current through them is called electrolysis. The current makes positive ions move to the negative terminal and negative ions to the positive. Electrolysis makes it possible to separate hydrogen from water.

Electrolysis

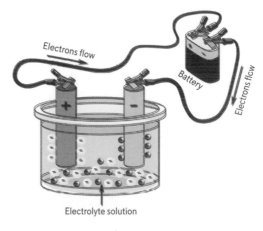

Electrons flow

Battery

Electrons flow

+

−

Electrolyte solution

WHAT IS **FLUORESCENCE?**

Fluorescence is the ability of a substance to glow. It occurs when a substance absorbs electromagnetic radiation or UV rays. Because of this, the energy levels of its electrons go up and then come back to the original levels. In this process it emits a photon which is visible to our eyes as a light or glow.

Amazing glow-in-the-dark body paint

Fluorescent light bulbs

HOW DOES A **FLUORESCENT LAMP WORK?**

A fluorescent lamp converts electrical energy into light energy. There is mercury gas inside the lamp. When an electric current passes through the gas, it energizes it and the gas produces ultraviolet radiation. This ultraviolet radiation makes the phosphor coating on the lamp's inner wall radiate bright light.

Big?

ARE **FLUORESCENCE AND PHOSPHORESCENCE THE SAME THING?**

Glow-in-the-dark moon and stars

Both fluorescence and phosphorescence are glows from a substance. In both cases, the glow or light is of a lower energy than the light that is absorbed. The main difference is the time it takes to emit the light. In fluorescence, the emission is almost immediate and it vanishes as soon as the source of electromagnetic or UV radiation stops—a fluorescent light bulb, for example. In phosphorescence, the substance can store the absorbed light energy for a longer time and continues to emit it later, resulting in an afterglow—like the glow-in-the-dark stars you put on the ceiling.

IS FLUORESCENCE USED IN MEDICAL RESEARCH?

Yes, it is widely used. For example, by using fluorescent dyes, scientists can study how our cells exchange protein. They use this dye on the protein of one cell and then, under UV light, track the movement and progress of that protein in its nearby cells.

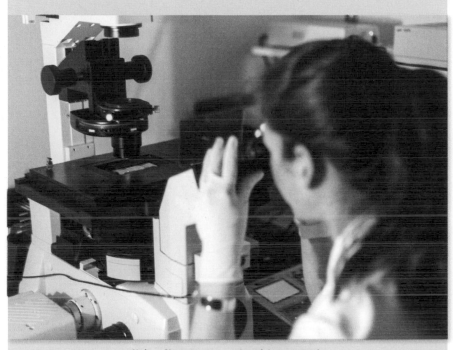

Using fluorescence to aid research

WHY DOES THE OCEAN GLOW AT NIGHT IN SOME COASTAL AREAS?

The glow comes from minute sea organisms that appear as tiny dots to our eyes. There is a chemical inside these organisms that starts glowing when oxygen is dissolved in the surrounding water. This is also called bioluminescence.

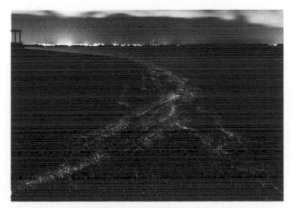

Bioluminescence

HOW DO DETERGENTS MAKE CLOTHES WHITER?

Fluorescent whitening substances are used in some detergents. As time passes, white clothes tend to become light yellow. Washing white clothes with these special detergents helps restore their whiteness.

Clothes washed in a fluorescent detergent

Rapid-FIRE ?

CAN MUSHROOMS GLOW?

Yes, some do. They grow in Vietnam and Brazil.

Glowing mushrooms

ARE GLOWING PIGS REAL?

They are, but they were created artificially by scientists using a fluorescent protein found in jellyfish DNA.

Jellyfish

WHICH FLUORESCENT COLOR ATTRACTS BEES MORE?

Fluorescent blue.

WHY IS CARBON SO IMPORTANT?

Carbon is the key element in the chemistry of life. Without carbon, life cannot exist. Carbon compounds are also important ingredients in a wide range of products that people use every day—from plastics and paint to food and medicines. These compounds also contain other elements, such as hydrogen, nitrogen, and oxygen.

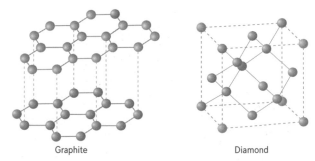

Granules of raw carbon

HOW MUCH **CARBON IS THERE IN THE UNIVERSE?**

It is the fourth most abundant element in the Universe.

Carbon exists all over the Universe.

WHICH FORM OF **CARBON DOESN'T HAVE A CRYSTALLINE STRUCTURE?**

Amorphous carbon.

WHICH IS THE SIMPLEST **HYDROCARBON COMPOUND?**

Methane.

IN WHAT FORMS DOES **CARBON NATURALLY OCCUR?**

Carbon takes on three different structural forms: diamond, graphite, and amorphous. In a diamond, one carbon atom is bonded with four other carbon atoms, making it the hardest substance ever known. The structure of graphite is layered. Graphite is black, very soft, and is a good conductor of electricity.

Graphite   Diamond

Molecular structure of graphite and diamond

WHAT IS THE CARBON CYCLE?

Carbon atoms constantly circulate from the atmosphere to Earth and back again. For example, animals breathe out carbon as carbon dioxide, plants absorb carbon dioxide from the air, organisms release carbon when they die, a fire releases carbon dioxide, the oceans absorb carbon and so on—this is the carbon cycle.

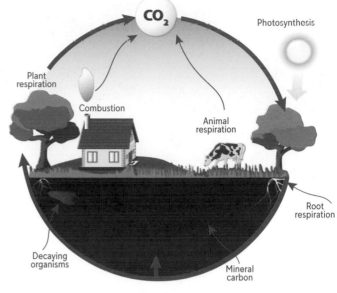

Carbon cycle

WHAT IS A CARBON CHAIN?

Carbon atoms often link together to form very long, thin molecules called a carbon chain. A common example is the molecules of propane, which consist of three carbon atoms in a row, with hydrogen atoms attached. Propane is commonly used as a fuel for engines and outdoor grills.

Cylinder of propane

Big? WHAT IS BLACK GOLD?

Formation of petroleum deposits

Petroleum is known as black gold, because of its color and the fact that it is expensive. It is basically a complex organic compound of hydrogen and carbon, formed from tiny plants and animals that lived in warm seas millions of years ago. These were buried beneath the seabed when they died and, as the seabed sediments hardened into rock, their remains were transformed into oil trapped in cavities in the rock. Gasoline, diesel, paraffin, petroleum jelly, and other substances are extracted from this raw oil.

HOW IS PLASTIC MADE?

Most plastics are made from ethene, a by-product of oil that is heated under pressure. During the process, ethene molecules bond together in long chains and become tangled. The stiffness of plastic depends on how these strands are held together.

Twisty straws and stiff pipes are both made of plastic.

WHAT ARE CRYSTALS?

Crystals are hard, shiny solids formed in regular geometric shapes. Grains of salt, sugar, and sand are all crystals, and so are diamonds. Each crystal is made up of a very regular structure of atoms, ions, or molecules. Crystallography is the study of crystals, usually using X-rays.

Crystal formation in pure quartz

WHAT IS THE DIFFERENCE BETWEEN DIAMONDS AND QUARTZ?

The shapes of diamonds and quartz crystals are very different from each other. Diamonds have eight-sided crystals of nearly the same width and length. Quartz crystals, on the other hand, have six-sided elongated crystals with only one terminating end. Each also has a different density.

Big? HOW MANY KINDS OF CRYSTALS ARE THERE?

There are four main kinds—covalent, ionic, metallic, and molecular. Covalent crystals are very strong and hard to break. Diamond and silicon are examples. Ionic crystals hold each other to form distinctive patterns. They are solid and have a high melting point. Table salt is an ionic crystal. Metallic crystals, such as gold, are made of metals. They shine and are good conductors of electricity. The fourth kind, molecular crystals, are defined by the arrangement of electrons between different hydrogen atoms. An example is dry ice.

Diamond and dry ice are both forms of crystals

IS DESERT ROSE A FLOWER?

Yes, but it is also the name for a crystal formation of gypsum in deserts. Gypsum rosettes form when there is a good amount of calcium sulfate in the ground. Gypsum loses water through evaporation, and a large prism or flat, plate-shaped, petal-like structure called a "desert rose" is formed.

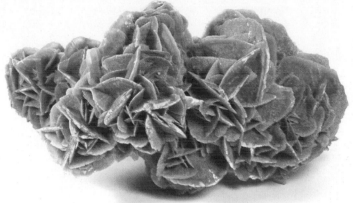

Desert rose

DO CRYSTALS FORM DUE TO HEAT?

When a solution is heated and the solvent starts evaporating, leaving behind the solute, the process is called crystallization. Crystals of the solute start forming on the surface after cooling. More crystals are formed if the cooling rate is fast, but slow cooling forms larger crystals.

Salt crystals

WHAT ARE PENCIL LEADS MADE OUT OF?

Raw graphite in crystal form

Graphite, which is found as a crystalline, natural form of carbon. A slightly altered form is produced by processing carbon-saturated molten iron and nickel.

Rapid-FIRE ?

CAN EVERYTHING BE CRYSTALLIZED?

Almost all solid things can be, including DNA.

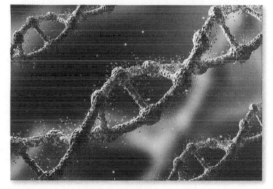

DNA

WHAT ARE THE LARGEST KNOWN CRYSTALS?

Cave of Crystals, Mexico

Giant selenium crystals in the Cave of Crystals in Chihuahua, Mexico. The largest is about 39 ft long—as tall as five Christmas trees!

IS GLASS A CRYSTAL?

No, most glass has jumbled-up molecules or atoms.

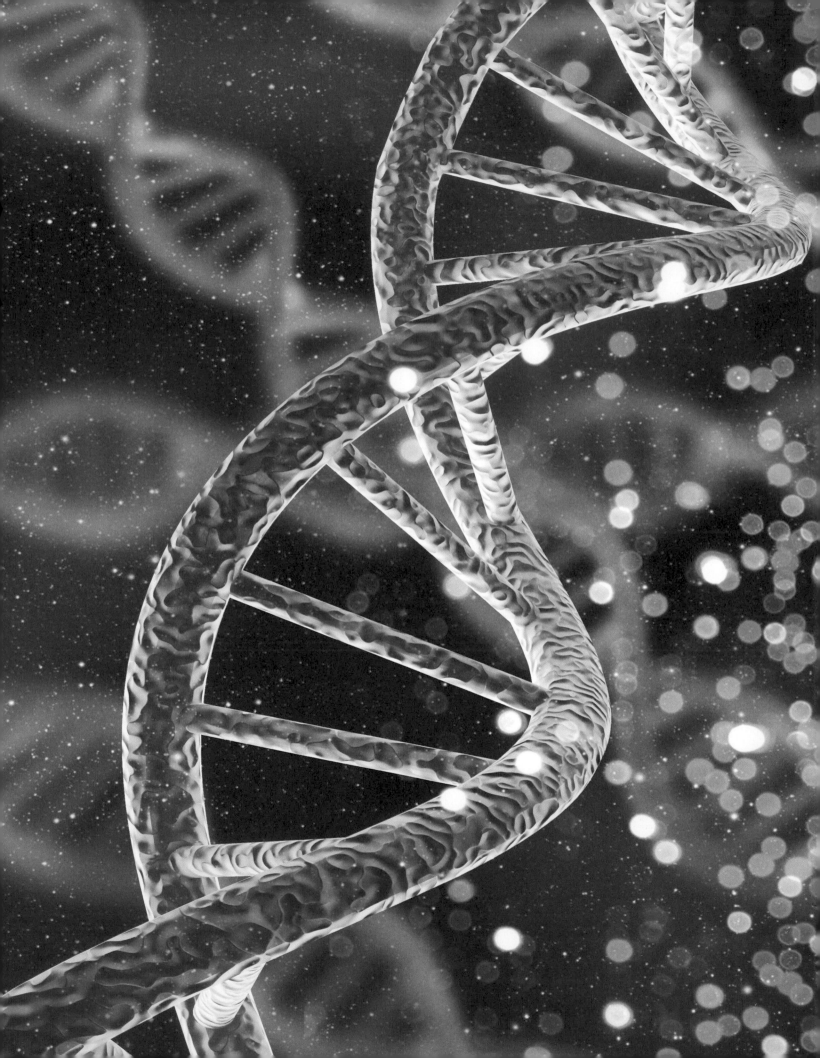